Commentary on Saint Paul's

First Letter to the Thessalonians

and

Letter to the Philippians

Aquinas Scripture Series Vol. 3

Revised Standard Version Bible Text

Commentary on Saint Paul's

First Letter to the Thessalonians

and the

Letter to the Philippians

by

St. Thomas Aquinas

Translated by
F.R. Larcher and Michael Duffy

MAGI BOOKS, INC.

33 Buckingham Dr.   Albany, N.Y. 12208

The Bible text in this publication is from the
Revised Standard Version of the Bible,
copyrighted 1946 and 1952 by the Division
of Christian Education of the National
Council of the Churches of Christ in the
U.S.A. and used by permission.

Brackets or parenthesis around a quotation indicate that it is from the
Vulgate.

These commentaries are divided into Lectures on each Chapter. Thus 2–2
indicates the second Chapter of the Scripture text, and the second Lecture
on this Chapter.

Library of Congress Catalog Card Number: 66–19306
SBN 87343–028–x

Manufactured in the United States of America by the
Hamilton Printing Co.

FIRST LETTER TO THE THESSALONIANS

TRANSLATED BY MICHAEL J. DUFFY, O.P.

The Thessalonians, who are here the object of Paul's praise and concern, were the citizens of Thessalonica. At this time, Thessalonica was an important, thriving city and the capital of Macedonia.

Paul established the church at Thessalonica during his second missionary journey. His success seems to have been quite notable, but he was eventually forced to flee the city under threat of bodily harm from unbelievers. His concern for the fate of his new Thessalonian converts prompted him to send Timothy to them. Timothy reported back that their faith remained unshaken, but that they had need of further doctrine and instruction. This first letter to the Thessalonians is Paul's response, and shows his joy over their constancy. Especially important is Paul's teaching on the Second Coming of Christ (the *parousia*.)

Paul wrote this first letter to the Thessalonians from Corinth, probably in the year 50–51. It is regarded as the first of his many letters.

Valuable information on the nature and characteristics of St. Thomas' biblical commentaries and their doctrinal and historical importance can be found in the general *Introduction* by Matthew L. Lamb, to his translation of the letter to the Ephesians in this same series.

1

PROLOGUE

The waters increased, and bore up the ark and it rose above the earth (Gen. 7:17).

These words are appropriate to the contents of this letter. The Church is symbolized by the *ark*, as is stated in I Peter 3, for as in the ark a few souls were saved, the others perishing, so also in the Church a few, that is, only the elect, will be saved.

The "waters" signify tribulations. First, because flooding waters strike like tribulations: "And the rain fell, and the floods came, and the winds blew and beat upon that house" (Matt. 7:25). Yet the Church is not shaken by the force of the floods; so Matthew adds, "but it did not fall."

Secondly, because water extinguishes fire: "Water extinguishes a blazing fire" (Sir. 3:30). Similarly, tribulations diminish the force of desires so that men do not follow them at will; but they do not diminish the true charity of the Church: "Many waters cannot quench love, neither can floods drown it" (Cant. 8:7).

Thirdly, because waters inundate by flooding: "Water closed over my head" (Lam. 3:54). Yet the Church is not overcome by them: "The waters closed in over me, the deep was round about me; weeds were wrapped about my head" (Jon. 2.6). And just before this, "Yet would I again look upon your holy temple."

Therefore, the Church is not destroyed but uplifted: first, by lifting the mind to God, as is clear from Gregory: "The evil things which bear down upon us here compel us to go to God." "And in their distress they seek me" (Ho. 6:1). Secondly, the Church is raised up through spiritual consolation: "When the cares of my heart are many, thy consolations cheer my

3

soul" (Ps. 94:19); "For as we share abundantly in Christ's sufferings, so through Christ we share abundantly in comfort too" (2 Cor. 1:5). Thirdly, the Church is upraised by increasing the number of the faithful; for God has spread the Church in time of persecution: "But the more they were oppressed, the more they multiplied and the more they spread abroad" (Ex. 1:12).

It seems then that these words are appropriate to this letter because the Thessalonians stood firm after suffering many tribulations. Let us, therefore, look at the text.

1–1

1 Paul, Silvanus and Timothy, to the church of the Thessalonians in God the Father and the Lord Jesus Christ: Grace to you and peace. 2 We give thanks to God always for you all, constantly mentioning you in our prayers, 3 remembering before our God and Father your work of faith and labor of love and steadfastness of hope in our Lord Jesus Christ. 4 For we know, brethren beloved by God, that he has chosen you; 5 for our gospel came to you not only in word, but also in power and in the Holy Spirit and with full conviction. You know what kind of men we proved to be among you for your sake. 6 And you became imitators of us and of the Lord, for you received the word in much affliction, with joy inspired by the Holy Spirit; 7 so that you became an example to all the believers in Macedonia and in Achaia. 8 For not only has the word of the Lord sounded forth from you in Macedonia and Achaia, but your faith in God has gone forth everywhere, so that we need not say anything. 9 For they themselves report concerning us what a welcome we had among you, and how you turned to God from idols, to serve a living and true God, 10 and to wait for his Son from heaven, whom he raised from the dead, Jesus who delivers us from the wrath to come.

The Apostle wishes to strengthen the Church in the face of tribulations. First, in the face of present tribulations, and Paul does this in the first letter to the Thessalonians. Secondly, Paul warns against tribulations to come in the time of the Antichrist, and he does this in the second letter to the Thessalonians.

The first letter is divided into the greeting and the message, which begins at the words, *we give thanks to God always for you all.* First, Paul mentions the people who send the greeting; secondly, the Church which is greeted; thirdly, his hope for blessings. It should be noted that since we are all equal if we do not fail in our duties, the Apostle, in writing to these good people, does not mention his title, but supplies only his humble name which is *Paul.* He also adds the names of two persons who preached to them with him: *Silvanus,* who is Sylas, and *Timothy,* whom he circumcised, as is mentioned in Acts 16.

Paul greets the Church, which is the assembly of believers, *in God the Father and the Lord Jesus Christ,* that is, in the faith of the Trinity and of the divinity and humanity of Christ, because our beatitude will consist in knowing them. He mentions only the person of the Father and the incarnate Son, in which two is understood the Holy Spirit who is the bond between the Father and the Son.

The blessings he asks are *grace,* which is the source of all good things: "But by the grace of God I am what I am" (1 Cor. 15:10); and *peace,* which is our end: for there is peace when desire is totally at rest.

Then when Paul says, *we give thanks,* he begins the letter's message: first, he commends them for their past perseverance; secondly, he urges them to act well even in the future (4:1). In addition, Paul first gives thanks in general for their blessings; secondly, he remarks upon their blessings in particular matters (1:4). In treating the first point he does two things. First, he offers thanksgiving; secondly, he indicates the reason for the thanksgiving (1:3). Again, Paul first gives thanks for them; secondly, Paul prays for them (1:26).

In treating the first point, Paul mentions three things that ought to be present in thanksgiving. First, thanksgiving should be directed to God: *we give thanks to God.* "He bestows favor and honor" (Ps. 84:11). "Every good endowment and every perfect gift is from above, coming down from the Father of lights" (Jas. 1:17). Thanksgiving should be unceasing; so Paul says, *always*. It should also be universal, so Paul says, *for you all;* and later Paul adds, *give thanks in all circumstances* (5:18).

Then he prays for them saying: *constantly mentioning you in our prayers;* as if saying: Whenever I pray I am mindful of you: "Without ceasing I mention you always in my prayers" (Rom. 1:9).

Then when he says, *remembering . . . your work of faith,* Paul mentions the blessings for which he offers thanks, that is, faith, hope, and charity: "So faith, hope, love abide, these three" (1 Cor. 13:13). First, he mentions faith because it is an essential condition for obtaining the things to be hoped for, a means of revelation not based on appearances: "For whoever would draw near to God must believe that he exists and that he rewards those who seek him" (Heb. 11:6). This, however, is not sufficient unless the person practices good works and makes an effort; so Paul says, *your work of faith and labor.* "Faith apart from works is dead" (Jas. 2:26). The person who gives up while laboring for Christ is worth nothing: "They believe for a while and in time of temptation fall away" (Lk. 8:13). Paul uses the words, *work* and *labor,* implying that he is mindful of their active and struggling faith.

Paul also gives thanks for the love in which they abounded. Later (4:9), he says: *but concerning love of the brethren you have no need to have any one write to you.*

Then he gives thanks for their *hope,* which enables them to endure sufferings patiently: "Rejoice in your hope, be patient in tribulation" (Rom. 12:12). In addition, Paul gives thanks for the *steadfastness* of their hope: "You have heard of the steadfastness of Job" (Jas. 5:11). Finally, Paul gives thanks for *hope in our Lord,* that is, the hope we have in Christ, or the hope Christ gave to us: "We have been born anew to a living hope through the resurrection of Jesus Christ from the dead" (1 Pet. 1:3). This hope is, *before our God,* not before the eyes of men; "Beware of practicing your piety before men in order to be seen by them" (Matt. 6:1). "We have this as a sure and steadfast anchor of the soul" (Heb. 6:19). For hope in the old dispensation did not lead to God.

Then when Paul says, *For we know, brethren beloved by God, that he has chosen you,* he recalls their blessings in particular matters. First, he congratulates them for having received the gospel devoutly and willingly in spite of tribulations; secondly, Paul congratulates them because they did not fall away from the gospel in time of trial (2:1). Again, the first part is divided into two. First, Paul points out the kind of preaching that had been given to them; secondly, he points out how this preaching was received by them (1:6). In treating the first point Paul does three things. First, he tells what he knew about them; secondly, he indicates the manner of his preaching (1:5); thirdly, he remarks upon what they knew about the Apostle (1:5).

So Paul says, *brethren, beloved by God,* not only generally, insofar as God gives existence to all of nature, but specifically, insofar as you are each called to an eternal reward: "Yet I have loved Jacob" (Mal. 1:3). "All those consecrated to him were in his hand" (Deut. 33:3). *He has chosen you,* as if implying: I am certain that you are among the elect, although you did not merit this election; rather you are freely chosen by God. And I know this because God granted me abundant evidence of this in preaching, that is, that those to whom I preach are chosen by God, for God gives them the grace to listen profitably to the word preached to them; or else, God gives me the grace to preach rewardingly to them.

What is said in Ezekiel (3:26) would seem to contradict this: "And I will make your tongue cleave to the roof of your mouth, so that you shall be dumb." To counter this Paul first calls to mind how powerfully he preached to them; secondly, he calls upon their own witness with the words: *you know* . . . Powerfully, because he came not in loftiness of speech, *but in power:* "And my speech and my message were not in plausible words of wisdom, but in demonstration of the Spirit and power" (1 Cor. 2:4). "For the kingdom of God does not consist in talk but in power" (1 Cor. 4:20). Now this may have reference either to the authentication of his preaching or to the manner of his preaching. If it is the first alternative, then Paul's preaching to them was authenticated not by arguments but by the power of signs, and so it is said in Mark (16:20): "The Lord worked with them and confirmed the message by the signs that attended it"; and by the giving of the Holy Spirit; so Paul says, *and in the Holy Spirit.* "While Peter was still saying this, the Holy Spirit fell on all who heard the word" (Ac. 10:44). "While God also bore witness by signs and wonders and various miracles and by gifts of the Holy Spirit" (Heb. 2:4). *And with full conviction.* Paul adds this so that they would not believe that they received less than the Jews, indicating that the Holy Spirit does not discriminate among persons; but that the preaching was in the same fulness among them as among the Jews: "And they were all filled with the Holy Spirit" (Ac. 2:4).

But if it is the second alternative, then *in power* seems to mean "showing you a virtuous life." "Jesus began to do and teach" (Ac. 1:1). *And in the Holy Spirit* who brings things to mind; "For it is not you who speak but the Spirit of your Father speaking through you" (Matt. 10:20). *With full conviction,* because I have instructed you in everything necessary for the faith. And he appeals to their testimony on this point when he says: *You know what kind of men we proved to be among you for your sake,* that is, what kind of gifts and powers we have exhibited among you: "I hope it is known also to your conscience" (2 Cor. 5:11).

Then when he says, *and you became imitators of us,* he shows how creditably they received his preaching and did not fall away in time of trial. First, Paul shows their excellence in that they have imitated others; secondly, because they made themselves an example to others (1:7). In treating the first point Paul does two things. First, he shows whom they have imitated; secondly, he shows in what things they have imitated them (1:6).

In treating the first point, Paul says that they have imitated the ones they should, namely, their prelates; so he says: *You became imitators of us,* "Brethren, join in imitating me" (Phil. 3:17); that is, you imitated me not in my human failings but in those points in which I have imitated Christ by patience in the midst of suffering: "If any man would come after me, let him deny himself and take up his cross and follow me" (Matt. 16:24). "Christ also suffered for you, leaving you an example, that you should follow in his steps" (1 Pet. 2:21). Therefore, Paul says, *in much affliction, with joy,* that is, although a considerable amount of tribulation threatened you because of the gospel, nevertheless you have accepted that with joy: "Count it all joy, my brethren, when you meet various trials, for you know that the testing of your faith produces steadfastness" (Jas. 1:2). "Then they left the presence of the council, rejoicing that they were counted worthy to suffer dishonor for the name of Jesus" (Ac. 5:41). *With joy,* Paul says, *inspired by the Holy Spirit* who is the love of God, and who imbues joy in those who suffer for Christ because they love Him: "If a man offered for love all the wealth of his house, it would be utterly scorned" (Cant. 8:7).

And you are our imitators to such an extent that you can be imitated by others; therefore he says: *so that you become an example to all the believers in Macedonia and in Achaia.* In making this point, Paul does three things. First, he shows that they can be imitated; secondly, he shows how their fame has spread (1:8); thirdly, Paul shows how they were praised by all peoples (1:9).

So Paul says: you have imitated us so perfectly that *you became an example,* that is, an example of life not only in your own surroundings, but in other places as well: "Let your light so shine before men, that they may see your good works and give glory to your Father who is in heaven" (Matt. 5:16). You became an example to all believers to whom your faith has become known. Your goodness was added to this, *for the word of the Lord sounded forth from you,* that is, the Lord has been preached; in other words, your fame was diffused not only in Macedonia and Achaia, who are your neighbors, *but your faith in God has gone forth everywhere,* that is, a faith which God accepts, which joins you to God, and which is edifying everywhere: "Your faith is proclaimed in all the world" (Rom. 1:8). And proof exists for all this, *so that we need not say anything.* It is the practice of a good preacher to use as an example the blessings coming to others: "Your zeal has stirred up most of them" (2 Cor. 9:2).

Then when Paul says: *for they themselves report concerning us,* he remarks on the praise which they had received from others, because, *they themselves report concerning us what a welcome we had among you.* A similar point is made in Prov. (31:31): "Give her of the fruit of her hands, and let her works praise her in the gates." Those who commend you praise my preaching and your conversion. *They themselves report concerning us what a welcome we had among you,* since our entry was visited with great difficulty and genuine tribulations; but they also praise your conversion.

Finally, Paul makes known how, from whom, and to what they have been converted. In regard to the first point Paul says: *and how you turned to God,* that is, how readily and completely. "Return to me with all your heart" (Joel 2:12). "Do not delay to turn to the Lord, nor postpone it from day to day (Sir. 5:7). In regard to the second point, Paul says, *from idols,* as is mentioned in 1 Cor. (12:2): "You know that when you were heathens, you were led astray to dumb idols." In regard to the third point he says, *to serve a living and true God* by the practice of adoration, not of creatures, but of God, which is in contrast with what is stated in Romans (1:25): "They worshipped and served the creature rather than the Creator, who is blessed forever." And Paul says, *living,* in order to exclude the cult of idolatry, because the idolators worshipped certain dead people whose souls they regarded as deified, such as Romulus and Hercules. And so Paul insists on *living.* "As I live forever" (Deut. 32:40). Also, since the Platonists considered some separate substances to be gods by participation, he says *true,* meaning, not by participation in the divine nature.

Since those who serve Him deserve a reward, and because this is the case with the Thessalonians, it remains for them to expect a reward; so Paul says to them, *to wait for his Son,* that is, God, descending *from heaven.* "Be like men who are waiting for their master to come home from the marriage feast" (Lk.

12:36). "Blessed are all those who wait for him" (Is. 30:18). These, however, are the men who girded their loins. We, however, are waiting for two things: first, for the resurrection, in order that we may clearly conform to Christ; hence Paul says: *whom he raised from the dead.* "He who raised Christ Jesus from the dead will give life to your mortal bodies" (Rom. 8:11). "Who will change our lowly body to be like his glorious body" (Phil. 3:21). Secondly, we are waiting to be freed from the punishment which awaits the guilty. For we shall be freed by Christ from sin, the cause of punishment. So Paul says: *Jesus who delivers us from the wrath to come.* "Hide us from the face of him who is seated on the throne, and from the wrath of the Lamb" (Rev. 6:16). No one can free us from this wrath but Christ: "Who warned you to flee from the wrath to come?" (Matt. 3:7).

2–1

1 For you yourselves know, brethren, that our visit to you was not in vain; 2 but though we had already suffered and been shamefully treated at Philippi, as you know, we had courage in our God to declare to you the gospel of God in the face of great opposition. 3 For our appeal does not spring from error or uncleanness, nor is it made with guile; 4 but just as we have been approved by God to be entrusted with the gospel, so we speak, not to please men, but to please God who tests our hearts. 5 For we never used either words of flattery, as you know, or a cloak for greed, as God is witness; 6 nor did we seek glory from men, whether from you or from others, though we might have made demands as apostles of Christ. 7 But we were gentle among you, like a nurse taking care of her children. 8 So, being affectionately desirous of you, we were ready to share with you not only the gospel of God but also our own selves, because you had become very dear to us. 9 For you remember our labor and toil, brethren; we worked night and day, that we might not burden any of you, while we preached to you the gospel of God. 10 You are witnesses, and God also,

how holy and righteous and blameless was our behavior to
you believers; 11 for you know how, like a father with his
children, we exorted each one of you and encouraged you
and charged you 12 to lead a life worthy of God, who calls
you into his own kingdom and glory.

Before, Paul commended the Thessalonians for having received God's word amid tribulations; now he praises them
because they did not fall away as a result of difficulties; in
mentioning this he does three things. First, he recalls their
troubles; secondly, Paul points out the kind of remedy he applied to them (3:1); thirdly, the reason for the praise is given
(3:8).

Paul said before that everybody talks about them and about
the role of the Apostle in their conversion. So Paul first treats
of his visit; secondly, of their conversion (3:13). In treating
the first point Paul does three things. First, he recalls the
perseverance which he had maintained before he came to them;
secondly, he recalls the sound character of the doctrine with
which he converted them (2:3); thirdly, he recalls the genuine
quality of his dialogue with the converts (2:10). Again, Paul
divides the first point into two parts. First, he mentions the
hardships which he had endured before he came to them;
secondly, how he did not lose his confidence as a result of
these hardships (2:2).

He remarks then: I say that other believers are telling of
our visit to you, which you are familiar with, for it *was not in
vain,* in the sense of not worry-free, but rather arduous in the
face of many hardships. Or perhaps, *not in vain,* in the sense
of not inconsequential but rather rewarding: "The earth was
without form and void" (Gen. 1:2). Or *not in vain,* meaning
not transitory but rather enduring. "I did not run in vain or
labor in vain" (Phil. 2:16).

But we had already suffered bodily trials: "Good sense
makes a man slow to anger" (Prov. 19:11): "Vigorous and
sturdy shall they be, declaring how just is the Lord" (Ps.
92:15). In addition to this, Paul suffered spiritual trials because
of injuries in Philippi, where he endured insults because of the

cure of the possessed woman. This city was in Macedonia. In spite of all this his confidence in his preaching was not diminished: "God is my salvation; I will trust, and will not be afraid" (Is. 12:2); rather it proved itself in preaching *to you the gospel of God in the face of great opposition* for your conversion: "He who presides, gives aid with zeal, with carefulness" (Rom. 12:8). "And, apart from other things, there is the daily pressure upon me of my anxiety for all the churches" (2 Cor. 11:28).

Then when he says: *for our appeal does not spring from error,* he shows the sound character of his preaching; and in showing this, Paul does two things. First, he exhibits the sound character of his doctrine; secondly, he explains certain matters he had remarked upon (2:4). In treating the first point, Paul does two things. First, he rules out the possibility of error in the doctrine; secondly, he imputes integrity to his doctrine (2:4).

A doctrine, however, may become corrupt either because of the matter taught or because of the teacher's intention. In relation to the first point, a doctrine may be corrupted in two ways: through error, for example, to teach that salvation is through Christ according to the Law: "Evil men and imposters will go on from bad to worse, deceivers and deceived" (2 Tim. 3:13). So Paul remarks, *our appeal does not spring,* like that of some, *from error.* Or the corruption may occur through adulteration, as is the case with those saying that one should indulge in pleasures. This teaching is derived from a certain Nicolaus who permitted promiscuous marriages and even gave his wife to others. So Paul adds, *or uncleanness:* "But I have this against you, that you tolerate the woman Jezebel, who calls herself a prophetess and is teaching and beguiling my servants to practice immorality and to eat food sacrificed to idols" (Rev. 2:20). "Is there any wrong on my tongue?" (Job 6:30).

Furthermore, his preaching is not *with guile* as it is with some who, though speaking the truth, nevertheless have a false intention; for they do not will the development of their listeners nor the honor of God, but they desire their own honor;

and against this Paul says: *nor with guile.* "Their tongue is a deadly arrow; it speaks deceitfully" (Jer. 9:8).

Thus his preaching is not tainted, but rather sound. But something is sound because it serves its nature. As a result, preaching is sound when someone teaches in that manner in which Christ taught; and so Paul says, *but just as we have been approved,* that is, in that manner and with that intention with which God chose and approved us for the preaching of the gospel, *so we speak.* "I had been entrusted with the gospel to the uncircumcised, just as Peter had been entrusted with the gospel to the circumcised" (Gal. 2:7). "For he is a chosen instrument of mine to carry my name before the Gentiles and kings and the sons of Israel" (Ac. 9:15).

Then when Paul says, *not to please men,* he shows that his preaching is not meant to be deceptive. First, by ruling out the manner in which it might appear to be misleading; secondly, by making this point evident through a sign (2:5); thirdly, he shows the same thing by reason of a causal consideration (2:5b).

In elaborating the first point Paul says: My preaching is not of such a nature that it is ultimately pleasing to men. [God has scattered the bones of those who please men" (Ps. 52:6).] "If I were still pleasing men, I should not be a servant of Christ" (Gal. 1:10). Sometimes, however, Paul and his companions sought to please men for the sake of God's glory, so that their preaching might be more fruitful, as is remarked in 1 Cor. (10:33): "Just as I try to please all men in everything I do, not seeking my own advantage, but that of many, that they may be saved." *But to please God who tests our hearts:* "All the ways of a man are pure in his own eyes" (Prov. 16:2). A sign of this, however, is that we did not employ flattery, that is, only speaking of pleasant things to them. "Do not deceive with your lips" (Prov. 24:28). "Prophesy not to us what is right; speak to us smooth things, prophesy illusions" (Is. 30:10).

And Paul makes the same point with a causal analysis. For someone wishes to please men for two reasons, that is, for the sake of advantages, or for the sake of glory; however, he excludes these from consideration here. He rules out the first possibility by saying: *for we never used words of flattery:* we avoided not only any flattery, but every occasion of *greed* as well: "There is great gain in godliness with contentment" (1 Tim. 6:6). "Every one is greedy for unjust gain" (Jer. 6:13). Then he rules out the other possibility when he says, *nor did we seek glory from men,* whether from you or from others, by reason of our teaching; although we might have been pampered, accepted favors and even been a burden to the Thessalonians, for they owed him attention and support. Thus Paul says, *though we might have made demands as apostles of Christ.* Paul terms it a demand because those preaching heretically to them sought to acquire favors from them beyond measure: "It is you who have devoured the vineyard, the spoil of the poor is in your houses" (Is. 3:14).

Then when Paul says, *but we were gentle [as children] among you,* he makes two points: first, that he is not desirous of human glory; secondly, that he does not wish to appear avaricious (2:9). In handling the first point Paul does two things. First, he gives evidence of his humility; secondly, he shows his concern by a simile (2:7).

Paul makes the first point by saying that *we were as children,* that is, humble. "If they make you master of the feast, do not exalt yourself; be among them as one of them" (Sir. 32:1). Then he employs the simile saying, *like a nurse taking care of her children,* who bends down to an infant and speaks to the stammering child, so that the child may learn to speak; the nurse even makes use of gestures: "I have become all things to all men" (1 Cor. 9:22); "As babes in Christ, I fed you with milk, not solid food" (1 Cor. 3:1). *So, being affectionately desirous of you, we were ready to share with you not only the gospel of God but also our own selves.* "The good shepherd lays down his life for the sheep" (Jn. 10:11). *Because you had become very dear to us.* "I will most gladly spend and be spent for your souls" (2 Cor. 12:15).

Then when Paul says: *for you remember our labor and toil,*

brethren, he proceeds in accordance with what he had said above, that is: *we never used . . . a cloak for greed,* for we have asked nothing of you, but an effort, *for you remember our labor and toil.* And some do indeed labor, but out of comfort seeking; but we do not labor in that manner, but rather with honest hard work. So Paul comments: *our labor,* not merely for the sake of discipline of the body, but with genuine toil. Therefore Paul adds, *you remember our toil.* Some people work during the day, but we in reality work *night and day.* By this remark Paul wishes to protect them from the misleading people who were over-receptive and also from the lethargic people among them: "And we labor, working with our own hands" (1 Cor. 4:12).

Then when Paul says: *you are witnesses,* he remarks on the orthodoxy of his discourse. First, he speaks about the sanctifying influence it may have on a person's life; secondly, he shows how full of concern his teaching was (2:11). So Paul remarks: *you are witnesses . . . how holy,* that is, how innocently, we conducted ourselves: "Be holy, for I am holy" (Lev. 11:44 and 19:2); *and righteous* toward our neighbor, as is made evident by "to live sober, upright and godly lives in this world" (Tit. 2:12); *and blameless was our behaviour to you believers,* which means that you believed because we have done nothing that could have caused anyone to be scandalized. *To you believers,* individually. It should be noted that sometimes a singular predication has considerable import.

Like a father, "For I became your father in Christ Jesus through the gospel" (1 Cor. 4:15); *we exhorted each one of you.* A similar example is found in Philemon (1:8): "Though I am bold enough in Christ to command you to do what is required, yet for love's sake I prefer to appeal to you." *And encouraged you,* through soft spoken words: "To comfort all who mourn; to grant consolation to those who mourn in Sion" (Is. 61:2). In contrast to this it is stated in Ezechiel (34:4) "With force and harshness you have ruled them."

And what were you told? *To lead a life worthy of God,* that is, that your conduct should be such that it might reflect favorably on the ministers of Christ. "To lead a life worthy of the

Lord, fully pleasing to him" (Col. 1:10). *Who calls you into his own kingdom and glory,* as is evident also in "Honor wisdom, that you may reign for ever" (Wis. 6:21).

2-2

13 And we also thank God constantly for this, that when you received the word of God which you heard from us, you accepted it not as the word of men but as what it really is, the word of God, which is at work in you believers. 14 For you, brethren, became imitators of the churches of God in Christ Jesus which are in Judea; for you suffered the same things from your own countrymen as they did from the Jews, 15 who killed both the Lord Jesus and the prophets, and drove us out, and displease God and oppose all men 16 by hindering us from speaking to the Gentiles that they may be saved—so as always to fill up the measure of their sins. But God's wrath has come upon them at last! 17 But since we were bereft of you, brethren, for a short time, in person not in heart, we endeavored the more eagerly and with great desire to see you face to face; 18 because we wanted to come to you—I, Paul, again and again—but Satan hindered us. 19 For what is our hope or joy or crown of boasting before our Lord Jesus at his coming? Is it not you? 20 For you are our glory and joy.

In what has gone before the Apostle disclosed the character of his coming to them; here he indicates the character of their conversion. In treating this Paul makes two points. First, he shows that they have been perfectly converted as a result of their steadfast faith; secondly, he shows how courageously they persevered amidst tribulations (2:14). Paul first remarks upon their blessings, for which he offers thanks, and then he supplies a reason for this.

So Paul says, *and,* since I have carefully preached to you, as a father to his children, *I* therefore *thank God* as a father does for the welfare of his children: "No greater joy can I have than this, to hear that my children follow the truth" (3 Jn. 1:3).

"With thanksgiving" (Phil. 4:6). But for what reason? *For this, that when you received the word of God which you heard from us, you accepted it not as the word of men but as what it really is, the word of God.* The preacher should give thanks when his preaching proves to be effective in the lives of his congregation. Paul tells them, *you heard the word of God from us,* that is, through us: "Let me hear what God the Lord will speak" (Ps. 85:8). "Faith comes from what is heard, and what is heard comes by the preaching of Christ (Rom. 10:17). *You accepted it,* that is, you kept it firmly in your heart, *not as the word of men;* for the words of man are empty: "You desire proof that Christ is speaking in me" (2 Cor. 13:3). "No prophecy ever came by the impulse of man, but men moved by the Holy Spirit spoke from God" (2 Pet. 1:21). And why does he give thanks? Because the fact that you have believed, God has worked in you. "For God is at work in you, both to will and to work for his good pleasure" (Phil. 2:13). "Thou hast wrought for us all our works" (Is. 26:12).

Then when he says, *for you, brethren, became imitators of the churches of God in Christ Jesus which are in Judea,* he shows how courageously they persevered in the midst of tribulations; and in treating this he makes two points. First, he speaks of their trials, in which they stood firm; secondly, of the remedy he proposes to apply (2:17). Again, the first point is divided into two parts. First, Paul commends them for their patience in the face of difficulties; secondly, he reprehends those responsible for the difficulties (2:15).

Consequently, Paul says: you received the word not as the word of men, *but as what it really is, the word of God,* for you exposed yourselves for its sake even to death. The fact that a man dies for the sake of Christ is testimony to the fact that the words of the faith are the words of God; and, therefore, "martyrs" means the same as "witnesses." *In Judea,* for it is there that the faith of Christ was first proclaimed: "For out of Zion shall go forth the law, and the word of the Lord from Jerusalem" (Is. 2:3). In addition, it was also there that the first persecution of the faith occurred, as is evident from Acts (8:1): "On that day a great persecution arose against the church in Jerusalem." "But recall the former days when, after you were enlightened, you endured a hard struggle with sufferings" (Heb. 10:32). The Thessalonians endured similar difficulties, so Paul remarks: *for you suffered the same things from your own countrymen,* that is, from the incredulous Thessalonians: "And a man's foes will be those of his own household" (Matt. 10:36).

Then when Paul observes, *who killed both the Lord Jesus,* he rebukes the Jews who started the persecution. First, he recalls their sin, and then the reason for the sin (2:16). In regard to the first point Paul does three things: first, he treats their sin in relation to God's ministers; secondly, with reference to God Himself; and thirdly as relating to the entire human race.

The ministers of God are those who preach, namely, Christ, the prophets and the apostles. Preaching is performed by Christ as the one from whom the doctrine originates, by the prophets who prefigured this doctrine, and by the apostles who carry out the injunction to preach.

Paul first makes reference to Christ when he says: *who killed the Lord Jesus,* as is clear from Matthew (21:38): "This is the heir; come, let us kill him." That it was the Gentiles who killed him is not a valid objection, for the Jews with their own words asked Pilate to kill him: "My heritage has become to me like a lion in the forest, she has lifted up her voice against me" (Jer. 12:8). Paul then speaks of the prophets when he mentions: *and the prophets.* "Which of the prophets did not your fathers persecute? And they killed those who announced beforehand the coming of the Righteous One, whom you have now betrayed and murdered" (Ac. 7:52). Paul next speaks of the apostles when he comments: *and drove us out,* that is, the apostles. "Beware of men, for they will deliver you up to councils, and flog you in their synagogues" (Mt. 10:17).

Secondly, Paul mentions the sin of the Jews in its relation to God, with the words: *and displease God,* although they may think that through this they do a service to God, as is evident in John 16. Actually, because they do not have zeal for God in accordance with knowledge, they are not pleasing to God, since they do not act in keeping with right faith and "without faith it is impossible to please him" (Heb. 11:6); "therefore the anger of the Lord was kindled against his people, and he stretched out his hand against them and smote them" (Is. 5:25).

Thirdly, Paul considers their sin in its relation to the whole human race, when he says: *and oppose all men.* "His hand against every man and every man's hand against him" (Gen. 16:12). And they are antagonistic, because they prohibit and impede the preaching to the Gentiles, and also the conversion of the Gentiles. In Acts 10 and 11 Peter is criticized for having gone to Cornelius; also in Luke 15 the elder son, the Jewish people, is disturbed because the younger son, the Gentile people, is received by the father. "Woe to him who says to a father, 'What are you begetting'" (Is. 45:10). "Would that all the Lord's people were prophets" (Num. 11:29).

The reason for this sin is found in the divine permission, by which God wills that they fill up the measure of their sins. Indeed, for all things which come about, either good or bad, there is a certain measure, because nothing is infinite; and the measure of all these things is in [God's] foreknowledge. The measure of good things is what it prepares, for "grace was given to each of us according to the measure of Christ's gift" (Eph. 4:7); the measure of evil things, however, is what it permits, for if some are evil, they are not as evil as they want, but as God permits. And, therefore, they live until they attain that which God permits: "Fill up, then, the measure of your fathers" (Matt. 23:32). So Paul says: *so as always to fill up the measure of their sins.* For after the suffering of Christ, God gave the Jews forty years to repent, but they were not converted; rather they multiplied their sins. God did not permit this to go on, so Paul states: *but God's wrath has come upon them until the end.* "For great is the wrath of the Lord that is kindled against us, because our fathers have not obeyed the words of this book, to do according to all that is written concerning us (2 Kg. 22:13). "For great distress shall be upon the earth and wrath upon this people" (Lk. 21:23). And you should not think that this wrath shall last for one hundred years only, but *until the end* of the world, when all the Gentiles will have embraced [the Christian religion], and then all of Israel shall be saved, as it appears from Rom. 10, Lk. 19:44, 21:6, and Matt. 24:2: "There will not be left here one stone upon another, that will not be thrown down."

Then when Paul says, *but since we were bereft of you, brethren, for a short time,* he shows the remedy that he proposed to apply for them, namely, that he will personally go to them. In regard to this he makes three points: first, he discusses his proposed visit; secondly he treats the obstacle to his visit (2:18); thirdly, he gives the reason why he wanted to go (2:19).

So Paul says: *but since we were bereft of you,* either on account of your tribulations, or because we were separated from you [*in conversation*], that is, missing the opportunity for conversation, and *in person,* that is, not being able to enjoy your company. Both of these things require the presence of a friend because it is consoling. But *not in heart,* for we are present in heart, as is evident from 1 Cor. (5:3): "For though absent in body I am present in spirit." *We endeavored the more eagerly and with great desire to see you face to face,* that we may be present also in body as we are in our heart; "I have longed for many years to come to you" (Rom. 15:23). When Paul says *we,* he intends a plural meaning, because he writes in the name of three persons, that is, in his own name, and that of Silvanus, and of Timothy. Therefore Paul says: *we wanted to come to you,* all of us perhaps once, but *I Paul, again and again,* that is twice, as I proposed; *but Satan hindered us,* that is, set up obstacles, perhaps through violent winds, as in: "Four angels standing at the four corners of the earth, holding back the four winds of the earth" (Rev. 7:1).

Then when Paul says: *for what is our hope,* he gives the reason for his proposal. First, in regard to the future; secondly, in regard to the present (2:20). Paul says: I desire to see you and I give thanks for your blessings which are our *hope;* for it is on account of these blessings that we hope for rewards from God, when He shall come to render to every one according to his deeds. For the greatest reward of the preacher comes from those whom he has converted. *Or joy,* because their joy is the

Apostle's joy, just as their goodness is the Apostle's goodness; for the goodness of the effect is accounted for by the goodness of the cause. *Or crown of boasting,* because as a result of their struggles he who encouraged them to struggle shall be decorated; for the commander who led the soldiers to combat is decorated: "He who disciplines his son will profit by him, and will boast of him among acquaintances" (Sir. 30:2). I ask what is this hope; *is it not you?* Yes, assuredly: in the future, that is, *before our Lord Jesus at his coming;* but also in the present, *for you are,* among all the faithful, *our glory:* "I would rather die than have any one deprive me of my ground for boasting" (1 Cor. 9:15); *and joy,* for which reason Paul rejoices over their good fortune in the present.

3–1

1 Therefore when we could bear it no longer, we were willing to be left behind at Athens alone, 2 and we sent Timothy, our brother and God's servant in the gospel of Christ, to establish you in your faith and to exhort you, 3 that no one be moved by these afflictions. You yourselves know that this is to be our lot. 4 For when we were with you, we told you beforehand that we were to suffer affliction; just as it has come to pass, and as you know. 5 For this reason, when I could bear it no longer, I sent that I might know your faith, for fear that somehow the tempter had tempted you and that our labor would be in vain. 6 But now that Timothy has come to us from you, and has brought us the good news of your faith and love and reported that you always remember us kindly and long to see us, as we long to see you—7 for this reason, brethren, in all our distress and affliction we have been comforted about you through your faith; 8 for now we live, if you stand fast in the Lord. 9 For what thanksgiving can we render to God for you, for all the joy which we feel for your sake before our God, 10 praying earnestly night and day that we may see you face to face and supply what is lacking in your faith? 11 Now may our God and Father himself, and our Lord Jesus, direct our way to you;

12 and may the Lord make you increase and abound in love
to one another and to all men, as we do to you, 13 so that he
may establish your hearts unblamable in holiness before our
God and Father, at the coming of our Lord Jesus with all his
saints.

Paul mentioned the trials they had endured and the relief
he intended to supply for them. Here he recalls how he came
to their assistance through the visit of Timothy. First, Paul
deals with the task of his messenger; secondly, Paul talks about
the contact established through Timothy (3:6); thirdly, Paul
writes on the effect of this contact on the Apostle (3:7). Paul
divides the first part into three parts. First, he mentions the
reason why he sent him; secondly, he mentions the person
whom he sent; thirdly, he speaks further about the reason for
sending him.

Paul comments: Therefore, although Satan hindered us, you
are still our glory, consequently, *when we could bear it no
longer,* that is, the influence of our love prompting us to go to
you: "They have become a burden to me, I am weary of bearing them" (Is. 1:14), and "Joseph could not control himself"
(Gen. 45:1), *we were willing,* Paul and Silvanus, *to be left
behind at Athens alone, and we sent Timothy,* who was the one
most in accord with the Apostle: "I have no one like him, who
will be genuinely anxious for your welfare" (Phil. 2:20). "I
sent to you Timothy, my beloved and faithful child in the
Lord" (1 Cor. 4:17). *Our brother,* sustained by charity. "A
brother helped by a brother is like a strong city" (Prov. 18:19),
and God's servant, for he is an important person in the Church:
"Are they servants of Christ? I am a better one" (2 Cor. 11:23).

And so Paul sends Timothy to strengthen the Thessalonians
and to report to Paul about them. When Paul says *to establish
you,* he shows that Timothy is sent to strengthen them. So
Paul first states this, and second the reason for the strengthening is stated (3:3). Paul says, *to establish and to exhort you,*
for the soul of a man is strengthened through encouragement:
"Your words have upheld him who was stumbling" (Job 4:4).
When you have turned again, strengthen your brethren (Lk.

22:32). And you are in need of encouragement *in your faith, that no one be moved by these afflictions.* "If the anger of the ruler rises against you, do not leave your place" (Ec. 10:4). And there is a twofold consideration strengthening them. The first is related to a divine ordination: *You yourselves know that this is to be our lot,* almost as if implying that God ordained that you shall enter into heaven through tribulations: "Through many tribulations we must enter the kingdom of God" (Ac. 14:22). "All who desire to live a godly life in Christ Jesus will be persecuted" (2 Tim. 3:12). Christ Himself traveled this path as is shown in Luke (24:46): "Was it not necessary that the Christ should suffer these things and enter into his glory?"

The other consideration strengthening them is a prediction concerning the future, for anticipated difficulties are less harmful. So Paul tells them: *for when we were with you, we told you beforehand that we were to suffer affliction,* that is, Paul had warned them about the tribulations they would go through in their time. *For this reason, when I could bear it no longer, I sent that I might know your faith,* how firm you are in your faith: "Know well the condition of your flocks, and give attention to your herds" (Prov. 27:23); *for fear that somehow the tempter had tempted you,* that is, the devil: "And the tempter came" (Matt. 4:3). There is a commentary which says: "Whose business it is to tempt."

But on the contrary, both the world and the flesh also tempt, as is seen in James (1:14): "Each person is tempted when he is lured and enticed by his own desire." Also in Genesis (22:1): "God tested Abraham." It is necessary to point out that "to tempt" means to make a test of something. And in this matter the purpose must be considered for which one wants to test something, and in what manner one wants to test something. For this occurs in two ways: either so that the person testing may know about it, or so that he may make it known to another. God does not need to tempt in the first way, for He knows what is in man as is stated in John 2. Rather in the second way: for God tempted Abraham so that others might know of his faith. A temptation in the first manner may occur in two ways, that is, it leads towards some good, as when the bishop examines those to be promoted; or else, somebody tempts in order to deceive, and this is the work of the devil; for the devil tests the condition of men in order that he may lead them to the various sins to which they are prone in accordance with their various dispositions: "Your adversary the devil prowls around like a roaring lion, seeking some one to devour" (Pet. 5:8). Therefore, it is the devil's business to tempt in order to deceive. The world and the flesh are said to tempt in a material way, for through them and the things to which they lead a knowledge is achieved about man as to whether he is really steadfast in God's commandments and in the love of God. Because if concupiscence triumphs, the person does not love God in a perfect manner, nor does he love in a perfect manner when the concerns of the world either frighten him or exert an undue influence upon him.

And that our labor would be in vain, because if you do not resist temptation our labor would be in vain: "I am afraid I have labored over you in vain" (Gal. 4:11). "None of the righteous deeds which he has done shall be remembered" (Ez. 18:24). The labor is regarded as "in vain" with respect to an eternal reward; nevertheless the good deeds performed prior to sin profit a person, for they shall live again after repentance, and also because they readily dispose one towards conversion.

Then when Paul says: *but now that Timothy has come to us from you,* he comments that Timothy spoke of their good practices towards God and towards the Apostle: *faith and love* towards God: "For neither circumcision counts for anything, nor uncircumcision, but a new creation" (Gal. 6:15); faith also towards the Apostle, so Paul says: *you always remember us kindly.* "The memory of Josiah is like a blending of incense prepared by the art of the perfumer" (Sir. 49:1). "The memory of the righteous is a blessing" (Prov. 10:7). *And reported that you long to see us, as we long to see you.* Augustine wrote: "Hardened is the soul that does not requite love, even if it does not wish to bestow it." "Look to Abraham your father and to Sarah who bore you" (Is. 51:2).

Then when Paul says: *we have been comforted about you,* he speaks of the threefold effect of their relationship, namely, of spiritual consolation, of the spirit of thanksgiving, in the words: *for what thanksgiving can we render to God for you,* and of the resultant frequent prayer, in the words: *praying night and day.* And so Paul tells them: because we have heard such things about you, we are encouraged, although the demands of temporal concerns are pressing, as well as bodily trials. "When the cares of my heart are many, thy consolations cheer my soul" (Ps. 94:19). "Blessed be the God and Father of our Lord Jesus Christ, the Father of mercies and God of all comfort" (2 Cor. 1:3). And this occurred *through your faith,* that is, having heard about the reliable character of your faith. *For now we live, if you stand fast in the Lord,* as if saying: I value your condition so highly that I think it sustains me: "It is enough; Joseph my son is still alive" (Gen. 45:28).

Then when Paul says, *for what thanksgiving can we render to God for you,* the second effect of their existent relationship is treated, namely, the spirit of thanksgiving, as if implying: I am not worthy to supply fitting thanks to God for you: "With what shall I come before the Lord?" (Mic. 6:6). "What shall I render to the Lord for all his bounty to me? (Ps. 116:12). However, the prayers of thanksgiving are offered *for all the joy;* a joy which is not entirely visible, but *which we feel for your sake* in our conscience *before our God* who beholds this; or perhaps *before God* in that those close to God please God: "Love does not rejoice at wrong, but rejoices in the right" (1 Cor. 13:6).

Then when Paul says, *night and day,* the third effect of their relationship is explained. First, he points out the frequency of his prayer; secondly, he shows what he desires while praying (3:11). So Paul insists: We give thanks for things past; nevertheless we do not fail to pray also for future concerns, indeed, [we do so] *night and day,* that is, in adversity and prosperity. "Evening and morning and at noon I utter my complaint and moan" (Ps. 55:17). *To supply what is lacking in your faith:* not matters that pertain to the fundamentals of the faith, but some special teachings which the Apostle did not preach to them at their [spiritual] birth: "I, brethren, could not address you as spiritual men, but as men of the flesh" (1 Cor. 3:1). "I have yet many things to say to you, but you cannot bear them now" (Jn. 16:12).

Then when Paul says: *may our God . . . direct our way to you*, he makes known what he desires for them; in regard to this he first shows what he is asking for (3:13). And Paul is asking for two things: One on his own behalf—that he may go to see them—and so he says: *may our God and Father himself, and our Lord Jesus, direct our way to you.* "I am ascending to my Father and your Father, to my God and your God" (Jn. 20:17). "The plans of the mind belong to man, but the answer of the tongue is from the Lord" (Prov. 16:1). The other is for their welfare, so Paul asks: *and may the Lord make you increase*, that is, in faith: "May the Lord add to his people a hundred times as many as they are" (1 Chr. 21:3). And Paul prays also that their merits may increase; so he says, *and abound in love*, which can always increase in this life: "Above all these put on love, which binds everything together" (Col. 3:14). And, first, charity *to one another*, secondly, charity *to all men*. "Let us do good to all men, and especially to those who are of the household of faith" (Gal. 6:10). And Paul gives an example of himself when he comments: *as we do to you*, as if to say: just as I also love you: "You are in our hearts, to die together and to live together" (2 Cor. 7:3).

But for what purpose does Paul pray? *So that he may establish your hearts unblamable in holiness*, that is, that nobody can complain about you; ". . . righteous before God, walking in all the commandments and ordinances of the Lord blameless" (Lk. 1:6). *In holiness before our God* who sees the heart: "In holiness and righteousness before him all the days of our life" (Lk. 1:75). And this shall be manifest *at the coming of our Lord Jesus*, that He may find you holy, who shall come *with all his saints;* that you might be in His presence, just as all the saints are before Him.

4–1

1 Finally, brethren, we beseech and exhort you in the Lord Jesus, that as you learned from us how you ought to live and

to please God, just as you are doing, you do so more and more.
2 For you know what instructions we gave you through the
Lord Jesus. 3 For this is the will of God, your sanctification:
that you abstain from immorality; 4 that each one of you know
how to take a wife for himself in holiness and honor, 5 not in
the passion of lust like heathen who do not know God; 6 that
no man transgress, and wrong his brother in this matter, because the Lord is an avenger in all these things, as we solemnly
forewarned you. 7 For God has not called us for uncleanness,
but in holiness. 8 Therefore whoever disregards this, disregards
not man but God, who gives his Holy Spirit to you. 9 But concerning love of the brethren you have no need to have any one
write to you, for you yourselves have been taught by God to
love one another; 10 and indeed you do love all the brethren
throughout Macedonia. But we exhort you, brethren, to do so
more and more, 11 to aspire to live quietly, to mind your own
affairs, and to work with your hands, as we charged you; 12 so
that you may command the respect of outsiders, and be dependent on nobody.

Earlier, the Apostle Paul commended the faithful for their
loyalty in the face of trials and for other good practices; here
Paul cautions them to act well in the future. First, Paul presents a general warning; secondly, Paul makes it more specific
(4:3). In regard to the first point, Paul does two things. First
he presents what he is intent upon; secondly, he indicates a
reason for the warning (4:1b). So Paul says: I heard about
your good practices of the past, but in the future we will continue to exhort you. So Paul prevails upon them, first, on his
own behalf when he remarks, *we beseech you,* "Pray for the
peace of Jerusalem" (Ps. 122:6). In addition, Paul prevails
upon them on behalf of Christ, and so he says, *and we exhort
you in the Lord Jesus.* And he exhorts them, because they are
holy: "Do not rebuke an older man but exhort him as you would
a father" (1 Tim. 5:1).

But what does Paul ask? *That as you learned from us how
you ought to live and to please God, just as you are doing, you*

do so more and more. The Apostle had taught them how they should conduct themselves in the practice of common justice, which is by keeping the precepts; that is why he says: *you learned from us how you ought to live.* "I will run in the way of thy commandments" (Ps. 119:32). Paul had also taught them how they might be pleasing to God in the practice of the counsels: "There was one who pleased God and was loved by him" (Wis. 4:10); or *how you ought to live,* that is, by virtuous actions. "Walk while you have the light" (Jn. 12:35); *and to please God* through the forming of good intentions. *Just as you are doing,* that is, that they might remain steadfast in the original teaching, without falling away from it: "But even if we, or an angel from heaven, should preach to you a gospel contrary to that which we preached to you, let him be accursed" (Gal. 1:8).

The reason for the warning is based on the benefit to be derived from heeding the warning; secondly, from the warning itself (4:2). Paul remarks: although you are good, nevertheless you shall grow markedly and improve through the repeated practice of the precepts and counsels. "God is able to provide you with every blessing in abundance" (2 Cor. 9:8). For charity is so encompassing that there will always be something left through which one might improve himself. Also, if difficulties are removed because of the warning, it is both proper and useful. "The law of the Lord is perfect, reviving the soul" (Ps. 19:7). "For the commandment is a lamp and the teaching a light, and the reproofs of discipline are the way of life" (Prov. 6:23). Paul then says: *what instructions,* that is, what kind of commandments, and he tells us that they are *through the Lord Jesus,* in that they are given through Him: "For I received from the Lord what I also delivered to you" (1 Cor. 11:23). "It was declared at first by the Lord, and it was attested to us by those who heard him" (Heb. 2:3). The precepts are as follows: *this is the will of God, your sanctification,* as if saying: All the commandments of God are for the purpose of making you holy; for sanctity means purity and constancy, and all of God's precepts lead thereto, so that a person may be cleansed from evil

and constant in good: "That you may prove what is the will
of God" (Rom. 12:2) which is made known through the precepts.

Then when Paul says: *that you abstain,* he warns them in
particular; and, first, he corrects them in regard to certain inordinate practices prevalent among them; secondly, he urges
them to maintain their virtuous actions (5:1). There were
three inordinate practices prevalent among them, namely, carnal vices among a certain number of them, curiosity, and an
inordinate grief for the dead. For these reasons Paul speaks
about these matters. About the second inordinate practice Paul
remarks in (4:9); the third inordinate practice he treats in
(4:13).

In treating the first inordinate practice he does two things.
First, he instructs them to refrain from the inordinate desire
for carnal things; secondly, he provides a reason for this (4:6).
And so he divides the first point into two. First, he forbids lust;
secondly, he forbids greed. He always associates these two, for
each one has reference to a corporeal object, although the latter
culminates in spiritual delight.

Paul first teaches them to beware of lust in regard to a woman
who is not their wife; secondly, in regard to one's own wife
(4:4). Therefore Paul insists, *that you abstain from immorality,*
for it is God's will to abstain from immorality. Therefore, it is
a mortal sin, for it is contrary to the commandment and the
will of God. "Beware, my son, of all immorality" (Tob. 4:12).
But also with regard to your wife, deny yourself honorably;
that each one of you know how to take [his vessel], that is his
wife, *in holiness,* denying yourself pleasure for a time, *and in
honor, not in the passion of lust,* that is, do not let passion be
the stimulus; *like heathen,* for it is characteristic of heathens to
desire immediate pleasures instead of those of the future life.
In holiness and honor, because this is the proper use of marriage, since it is for the good of the offspring or for fulfilling
an obligation; and so marriage may be without sin. But sometimes a venial sin is involved, if concupiscence is not exercised
beyond the limits of marriage, that is, when, although having
concupiscence, a person does not indulge it except with his

own wife. But when this takes place outside the bonds of marriage, the action becomes a mortal sin; and this happens when he would perform the action, even if she were not his wife, and more willingly with another woman. "Let marriage be held in honor among all, and let the marriage bed be undefiled; for God will judge the immoral and adulterous" (Heb. 13:4). "Likewise you husbands, live considerately with your wives, bestowing honor on the woman as the weaker sex, since you are joint heirs of the grace of life, in order that your prayers may not be hindered" (1 Pet. 3:7).

Then when Paul says, *that no man transgress,* he forbids greed, and insists *that no man transgress,* that is, no one should exert violence by taking another's property through brute strength. "Is it not the rich who oppress you?" (Jas. 2:6). *And wrong his brother* through fraud. "Like a basket full of birds, their houses are full of treachery" (Jer. 5:27).

When Paul says: *because the Lord is an avenger in all these things,* the reason for the warning is mentioned. First, Paul attributes it to the divine vengeance; secondly, he shows that this vengence is justifiable (4:7). Paul exhorts them to refrain from these things, for *the Lord is an avenger.* "I warn you, as I warned you before, that those who do such things shall not inherit the kingdom of God" (Gal. 5:21). For God certainly takes vengeance justly. One reason for this is that God has called us, and a second reason is that such actions are contrary to God's gifts to us. If the Lord calls you to one thing and you do something contrary, then punishment is due. So Paul points out that *God has not called us for uncleanness.* "As he chose us in him before the foundation of the world, that we should be holy and blameless before him" (Eph. 1:4). "Those whom he predestined he also called" (Rom. 8:30). And so Paul concludes: *therefore, whoever disregards this, disregards not man but God,* as if saying: This is the one special reason that I mentioned. The other reason is that these vices are opposed to the Spirit who was given to us. And he who does these things offends the Holy Spirit; so Paul says, *who gives his Holy Spirit to you.* "A man who has violated the law of Moses dies without mercy at the testimony of two or three witnesses. How much

worse punishment do you think will be deserved by the man
who has spurned the Son of God, and profaned the blood of
the covenant by which he was sanctified, and outraged the
Spirit of grace?" (Heb. 10:28).

Then when Paul remarks: *But concerning love of the brethren you have no need to have any one write to you,* he dis-
courages them from remaining idle. It should be realized, as
Jerome says in the letter to the Galatians, that the Thessalonians
were generous, and that it was the custom among the rich to
give away a great deal; as a result the poor idly depended on
their benefits without looking for work, but rather wasted time
in their homes. And so Paul first commends the generosity of
the donors, but he is then critical of the idleness of the recipi-
ents of the welfare (4:11). And first then, Paul adds that they
do not need to be reminded of the need for charity, but secondly he also advises that they make progress in it (4:10).
Paul observes, *but concerning love of the brethren,* that is, in
regard to your love for your brothers, *you have no need to have
any one write to you.* "Love one another with brotherly affection" (Rom. 12:10). "Let brotherly love continue" (Heb. 13:1).
And the reason for this is that, *you yourselves have been taught
by God,* that is, through the precept in the Law: "You shall
love your neighbor as yourself" (Lev. 19:18). Also, it is clear
from the gospel of St. John (13:34) "A new commandment I
give to you, that you love one another; even as I have loved
you." Or, *you yourselves have been taught* this by an interior
teaching, as is found in John (6:45): "Every one who has
heard and learned from the Father comes to me." And this
lesson is gained through the help of the Holy Spirit.

When Paul says: *but we exhort you, brethren, to do so more
and more,* he is urging them to make progress in charity. He
seemingly insists that since you have charity towards all men,
we urge you to make progress in it. And though others may
ridicule you, nevertheless devote yourself to charity: "In the
house of the righteous there is much treasure" (Prov. 15:6).

Paul next says: *aspire to live quietly.* He is correcting the
idle. First, he criticises their idleness; secondly, he indicates
how they ought to curtail it; and finally, he provides a reason

why they ought to curtail it. He says therefore, *aspire to live quietly.* ". . . loud and wayward, her feet do not stay at home" (Prov. 7:11). "We were not idle when we were with you, we did not eat any one's bread without paying, but with toil and labor we worked night and day, that we might not burden any of you" (2 Thess. 3:7). Paul desires that they combat idleness by performing daily tasks; hence he remarks: *to mind your own affairs.* "Prepare your work outside, get everything ready for you in the field; and after that build your house" (Prov. 24:27).

Paul specifies *your own affairs.* Does this mean that they should take no part in other's affairs? If so, he would be opposing what is clear in Romans (16:2) "Help her in whatever she may require from you." I elaborate by pointing out that things occur in a disorderly manner if they are not governed within the limits of reason, for example, when somebody drives himself excessively; they occur in an orderly manner if the dictates of reason are observed in regulating them. The latter is commendable.

To work with your hands. "Idleness teaches much evil" (Sir. 33:27). "This was the guilt of your sister Sodom: she and her daughters had pride, surfeit of good, and prosperous ease, but did not aid the poor and needy" (Ez. 16:49). And this is a precept for all those who have no other means of getting the things which enable them to live properly; for it is a law of nature that man care for his body. "If any one will not work, let him not eat" (2 Thess. 3:10). Now, there are two reasons for this. The first one comes from the duty to set an example for others; so Paul says: *so that you may command the respect of outsiders.* For the unbelievers see your idle life and they detest you. "He must be well thought of by outsiders, or he may fall into reproach and the snare of the devil" (1 Tim. 3:7). The second reason comes from the fact that you should not covet those things that belong to others, and so it is said, *and be dependent on nobody.* "The desire of the sluggard kills him" (Prov. 21:25). "Let the thief no longer steal but rather let him labor" (Eph. 4:28). And therefore, if this idleness is overcome, it will result both in good example and in the repression of desire.

4–2

13 But we would not have you ignorant, brethren, concerning those who are asleep, that you may not grieve as others do who have no hope. 14 For since we believe that Jesus died and rose again, even so, through Jesus, God will bring with him those who have fallen asleep. 15 For this we declare to you by the word of the Lord, that we who are alive, who are left until the coming of the Lord, shall not precede those who have fallen asleep. 16 For the Lord himself will descend from heaven with a cry of command, with the archangel's call, and with the sound of the trumpet of God. And the dead in Christ will rise first; 17 then we who are alive, who are left, shall be caught up together with them in the clouds to meet the Lord in the air; and so we shall always be with the Lord. 18 Therefore comfort one another with these words.

In what went before Paul aimed at bringing them to the practice of continence in place of their concupiscence, and at curtailing their idleness. Now he urges them to lessen their inordinate sorrow. First, he provides a warning; secondly, he assigns a reason for the warning (4:13b). Therefore, he forbids them to indulge in inordinate sorrow when he tells them, *you may not grieve*. It seems, though, that the Apostle views sorrow for the dead benignly. Nevertheless, he cautions them not to grieve overmuch, *as others*. Someone who grieves for the dead does possess compassion. A person grieves first because of the dissolution of the frail body; for we ought to take care of the body for the sake of the soul. "O death, how bitter is the reminder of you to one who lives at peace among his possessions" (Sir. 41:1). Secondly, a person grieves because of the separation and departure which is so painful to friends. "Surely the bitterness of death is past" (1 Sam. 15:32). Thirdly, we mourn because death reminds us of our own sin. "For the wages of sin is death" (Rom. 6:23). Fourthly, because death reminds us of our own death. "For this is the end of all men, and the living will lay it to heart" (Ec. 7:2). So moderate sorrow is permitted. "Weep less bitterly for the dead, for he has attained rest" (Sir. 22:11). Therefore, he says, *as others do who have no hope*, that is, because these people believe that these negative aspects of death are eternal; but we do not believe so. "Our commonwealth is in heaven, and from it we await a Savior, the Lord Jesus Christ, who will change our lowly body to be like his glorious body" (Phil. 3:20). So he says clearly, *concerning those who are asleep*. "Our friend Lazarus has fallen asleep" (Jn. 11:11).

A person who decides to go to sleep does three things. First, he lies down with the hope of eventually getting up: "Shall he that sleeps not rise again from where he lies" (Ps. 40:9). A person who passes away abiding in the faith feels the same way. Secondly, the soul in a sleeping person remains vigilant. "I slept, but my heart was awake" (Cant. 5:2). Thirdly, after sleep a man gets up much more refreshed and restored. In this same manner the saints will rise incorruptibly, as we read in 1 Cor. 15.

Then when Paul says, *for since we believe*, he provides a reason for the warning he had given. First, he establishes the resurrection; secondly, he rules out the faint suspicion of a delay (4:15); thirdly, he outlines the order of resurrection (4:16). It should be realized that the Apostle constructs the case for our resurrection on the basis of the resurrection of Christ (1 Cor. 15), for Christ's resurrection is the cause of our resurrection. So Paul makes his point here by a causal analysis. Christ's resurrection is not only the cause but also the pattern of our resurrection. The Word made flesh revives our bodies, while the Word as such revives our souls. Christ is the pattern of our resurrection in that Christ assumed flesh, and also rose embodied in flesh.

Nor is Christ only the pattern; He is also the efficient cause of our resurrection, for the things done by Christ's humanity were done not only by the power of His human nature, but also by virtue of His divinity united in Him. Just as His touch cured the leper as an instrument of His divinity, so also Christ's resurrection is the cause of our resurrection, not merely because it was a body that arose, but a body united to the Word of life. So the Apostle, firmly presupposing this, declares, *for since we*

*believe that Jesus died and rose again, even so, through Jesus,
God will bring with him those who have fallen asleep* [*those
who have fallen asleep through Jesus*]. Those have slept
through Jesus who were conformed to His death through baptism; or he says *through Jesus,* because God will bring them
with Him, that is, with Christ Himself. "The Lord your God
will come, and all the holy ones with him" (Zech. 14:5). "The
Lord enters into judgment with the elders and princes of his
people" (Is. 3:14).

Then when he says, *for this we declare to you by the word
of the Lord,* he rules out a delay in regard to the resurrection,
as if saying: We know that they shall rise and shall come with
Christ; therefore, we ought not to grieve so much. For those
who shall be found alive will not achieve the glory of resurrection before those who are dead. And for this reason he says:
for this we declare to you, not as the conjecture of a man, but
by the word of the Lord, whose words do not fail. *That we
who are alive,* that is, those who are living, shall not receive
the consolation accompanying the coming of Christ before the
dead. As a result Paul says, *we who are alive, who are left until
the coming of the Lord, shall not precede those who have fallen
asleep.*

It would seem to those who do not fully understand what
the Apostle is saying here that all this shall come about while
the Apostle is still alive; it seemed this way to the Thessalonians. Because of this misunderstanding he wrote them a
second letter in which he says: "Now concerning the coming
of our Lord Jesus Christ . . . we beg you, brethren, not to be
quickly shaken in mind or excited, either by spirit or by word,
or by letter purporting to be from us, to the effect that the day
of the Lord has come" (2 Th. 2:2).

But he is not talking at present about himself and his con-
temporaries, but about those who shall be found alive at the
time of Christ's coming. *We who are left,* that is, those who
shall be left after the persecution of the Antichrist, *shall not
precede those,* that is, those who are living shall not receive
their consolation first. "In a moment, in the twinkling of an
eye, at the last trumpet" (1 Cor. 15:52).

Then when he says, *for the Lord himself will descend from heaven,* he shows the order and manner of the resurrection. First, he discusses the cause of the resurrection; secondly, he presents its order and manner (4:16); thirdly, he ends with a consideration of their mutual consolation (4:18).

He proves his first point by saying, *the Lord himself.* It should be noted here, as was already mentioned before, that the cause of the general resurrection is Christ's resurrection. But if you should say: since it has already occurred (that is the resurrection of Christ), why does not its effect follow? I would reply to this by saying that it is the cause of our resurrection according to the activity of the divine power. God, however, acts according to the order of His wisdom. Therefore, our resurrection will occur when the order of divine wisdom shall determine it.

In order to prove that Christ is the cause of the resurrection, he shows that all the dead shall rise in the presence of Christ. Three causes cooperate in the accomplishment of the general resurrection: the principal cause is the divine power; the second cause is instrumental, that is, the power of the humanity of Christ. The third cause might be termed a ministering cause in that the power of the angels will have some effect in the resurrection. For Augustine shows that the things that occur now by virtue of corporeal creatures actually occur through God, by their mediation. In the resurrection, some things shall be done through the angels, such as the collection of the dust. But the restoration of the bodies and the soul's reunion with the body will be accomplished immediately through Christ.

Paul then presents these three causes. First, he sets forth the glorious humanity of Christ when he says, *the Lord himself.* "Jesus . . . will come in the same way as you saw him go into heaven" (Ac. 1:11). *With a cry of command.* In the first coming, he came as obedient. "He became obedient unto death" (Phil. 2:8). And that happened because it was the coming of humility; but this one will be the coming of glory. "Coming . . . with power and great glory" (Lk. 21:27).

Secondly, he presents the power of the angels when he says, *with the archangel's call,* not that anything is done by his voice, but rather by his ministry. He says, *archangel's* for all angels minister to the Church under one archangel. "This is Michael, the prince of the Church" (Rev. 12). [There is no accepted text that has this reading for a verse in the 12th chapter of the Revelation.] Or perhaps, *with the archangel's call,* that is, Christ's, Who is Prince of the angels. "Wonderful Counselor" (Is. 9:6). And the resurrection shall be through Christ's voice, corporeal or spiritual. "(They) shall hear the voice of the son of God" (Jn. 5:28); in other words, the dead shall rise and come to judgment, and they shall obey the bodily voice.

Thirdly, he considers the divine power when he says, *with the sound of the trumpet of God.* This is the divine power which is referred to as the voice of the archangel insofar as it will act through the ministry of the archangel. It is called the trumpet of God since the resurrection does come about by divine power. It is called a trumpet because of its resonance, which is derived from God who raises the dead.

In addition, the trumpet, which had many uses in the Old Testament, brings people together for war: "And creation will fight alongside him" (Wis. 5:20). The trumpet was also used for celebrations, as it will be employed in the heavenly Jerusalem. In addition, the trumpet was used for deploying the armies; in this way holy men assisted in the movement of troops. And so if it is a sound that you can hear, it is called a trumpet; but if it is not a sound, then it is the divine power of Christ present and manifest to the whole world.

Then when Paul says, *and the dead in Christ will rise first,* he mentions the order that the resurrection will follow. In doing so he makes three points. First, he treats the resurrection of the dead; secondly, he considers the meeting of the living with Christ (4:17); finally, he refers to the happiness of the saints with Christ (4:17b).

Because of these words some people believed that the last people alive would never die, as Jerome mentions in his letter. For Paul has said, *then we who are alive . . . shall be caught up together.* It might seem that there would be no other reason for distinguishing the living from the dead. But on the contrary: ["We shall all indeed rise"] (1 Cor. 15:51). "For as in Adam all

die, so also in Christ shall all be made alive" (1 Cor. 15:22).
"So death spread to all men" (Rom. 5:12).

And so I say that some shall be alive at the time when Christ
shall come for judgment, but in that moment they shall die and
immediately afterwards they will rise. Because of the minimal
time involved they are regarded as living. But then another
problem presents itself because it is said: *and the dead in Christ
will rise first* and *then we who are alive.* So it seems that the
dead will rise before the living will meet Christ, and that the
living will die when they meet Him. So it appears that some
will rise ahead of these others, and that there will not be a
resurrection of everyone at the same time. This is contrary, however, to what is found in 1 Cor. (15:22): "In a moment, in the
twinkling of an eye, at the last trumpet."

I wish to point out that there are two opinions on this matter.
For some say that the resurrection will not take place at the
same time for everybody, but that first the dead will come with
Christ, and during the time that Christ is coming the living
will be taken up into the clouds and they will die and rise while
they are being taken up. So that what is said to happen in a
moment may be understood as occurring in a brief amount of
time. And if you insist that it will happen in an instant, then
it should not be applied to the total resurrection of all, but
rather to the resurrection of individuals, for every individual
will rise in an instant. But there are others, who maintain that
everyone will rise at the same time and in an instant. They feel
that where Paul says *will rise first,* he denotes the order of
dignity, not the order of time. This does seem difficult to maintain for many still alive will suffer in the persecution of the
Antichrist and be more distinguished than those who had died
before.

And so it seems necessary to answer the question in a different way, saying that all will die and all will rise at the same
time. For the Apostle does not say that the dead will rise
first and then the living, but that the dead will rise before
the living will meet Christ. Therefore he is not speaking about
the resurrection in terms of the order in which they shall rise,

but of the order in which they will be taken up to meet Christ. For when the Lord does come, first those who are found alive will die and then, immediately together with those who had died before, they will rise up and be taken up into the clouds to meet Christ, as Paul clearly says.

But there is a difference between the good and the evil people, because the evil people will remain on the earth that they loved, while the good people will be taken up to the Christ whom they had sought. "Wherever the body is, there the eagles will be gathered together" (Matt. 24:28). In the time of the resurrection the saints will be conformed to Christ, not only with regard to the glory of the body (Phil. 3), but also with respect to place, for Christ will be in a cloud. "A cloud took him out of their sight" (Ac. 1:9), and "Jesus will come in the same way as you saw him go into heaven" (Ac. 1:11). And so the saints too will be taken up into the clouds.

The reason for this is to show their likeness to God. For in the Old Testament the glory of the Lord appeared in the form of a cloud. [The Lord said that he would dwell in a "cloud"] (1 Kg. 8:12). These clouds will be prepared by divine power in order to show the glory of the saints. Or, the resplendent bodies of the glorified will appear as clouds to the evil people who will remain on earth. "Behold, the bridegroom! Come out to meet him" (Matt. 25:6).

Then when Paul says, *and so we shall always be with the Lord,* he shows the beatitude of the saints, for they shall always be with the Lord and derive constant enjoyment from Him. "I will come again and will take you to myself, that where I am you may be also" (Jn. 14:3). The saints desire this: "My desire is to depart and be with Christ" (Phil. 1:23).

Then when he says, *therefore comfort one another with these words,* Paul concludes that they should comfort one another about the dead. He feels that since the saints will rise without suffering any loss, the Thessalonians should comfort one another about the dead. "Comfort, comfort my people, says your God" (Is. 40:1).

1 But as to the times and the seasons, brethren, you have no need to have anything written to you. 2 For you yourselves know well that the day of the Lord will come like a thief in the night. 3 When people say, "There is peace and security," then sudden destruction will come upon them as travail comes upon a woman with child, and there will be no escape. 4 But you are not in darkness, brethren, for that day to surprise you like a thief. 5 For you are all sons of light and sons of the day; we are not of the night or of darkness. 6 So then let us not sleep, as others do, but let us keep awake and be sober. 7 For those who sleep sleep at night, and those who get drunk are drunk at night. 8 But, since we belong to the day, let us be sober, and put on the breastplate of faith and love, and for a helmet the hope of salvation. 9 For God has not destined us for wrath, but to obtain salvation through our Lord Jesus Christ, 10 who died for us so that whether we wake or sleep we might live with him. 11 Therefore encourage one another and build one another up, just as you are doing. 12 But we beseech you, brethren, to respect those who labor among you and are over you in the Lord and admonish you, 13 and to esteem them very highly in love because of their work. Be at peace among yourselves.

In what he had written before, Paul corrected them in matters which needed to be improved upon, and now he begins to instruct them concerning the future. He first gives them a warning and then provides a prayer with the words, *may the God of peace himself sanctify you wholly.* These two things are indeed necessary for us. For the good deeds that we do are the result of free will, and so a man could profit from a warning. And since these deeds are also the result of grace, man needs prayer as well.

Concerning the first point he does two things: Paul first urges the Thessalonians to prepare themselves for the coming judgment; secondly, he shows them how they should prepare themselves (5:11). In addition, he divides the first part into two:

he points out a feature of the coming judgment and then he shows in what manner they ought to prepare themselves for the judgment (5:6). There is also a subdivision of the first section into two further parts that include this feature of the coming judgment and then an explanation (5:3). In the first part Paul puts to rest their concern for knowledge about the future coming, and then treats what they did know about it (5:2).

First then, Paul says it was necessary for me to write about the preceding matters because you needed to know about them. *But as to the times*, that is, of summer, winter, or rather of what the future times will be, it was not necessary to write. Because certain of these things are reserved for only the divine knowledge: "But of that day or hour no one knows, neither the angels in heaven, nor the Son, but only the Father" (Mk. 13:32). "It is not for you to know times or seasons which the Father has fixed by his own authority" (Ac. 1:7). "The more words, the more vanity, and what is man the better? For who knows what is good for man while he lives the few days of his vain life, which he passes like a shadow? (Ec. 6:11). And so it is not necessary to write about this, *for you yourselves know* what ought to be known, *that the day of the Lord will come like a thief in the night.*

In fact, all days depend on the Lord: "By thy appointment they stand this day" (Ps. 119:91). But this day especially belongs to the Lord, because His will is fulfilled in everyone: it is accomplished in the good people who are led to salvation as an end foreknown by God: "Who desires all men to be saved and to come to the knowledge of the truth" (1 Tim. 2:4); and in the evil people that are punished: "At the set time which I appoint I will judge with equity" (Ps. 75:2).

It will come like a thief, that is, unannounced: "If the householder had known at what hour the thief was coming, he would have been awake" (Lk. 12:39). "The day of the Lord will come like a thief" (2 Pet. 3:10). "I will come like a thief" (Apoc. 3:3). But why is it said that the day shall come during the night? It should be understood that both are involved because He comes during the day for the uncovering of our hearts: "Before the

Lord comes, who will bring to light the things now hidden in darkness and will disclose the purposes of the heart" (1 Cor. 4:5); but He comes at night because of the surprise element: "Behold, the bridegroom! Come out to meet him" (Matt. 25:6). Actually, it is not certain at what hour it will occur.

Then when he says: *When people say 'There is peace and security,'* he explains the things he had mentioned. First he refers to the evil people; secondly, to the good people (5:4). In regard to the first division he does two things. He first describes the false confidence of the evil people and secondly he refers to the danger of a delay. So Paul says: *the Lord will come like a thief,* because He shall come unexpectedly: *When people say 'there is peace,'* they shall be deceived in regard to the present time when they are living tranquilly: "But they live in great strife due to ignorance, and they call such great evils peace" (Wis. 14:22). *Security* has reference to the future: "Soul, you have ample goods laid up for many years; take your ease, eat, drink, be merry" (Lk. 12:19).

But in contrast: "Men fainting with fear and with foreboding of what is coming on the world" (Lk. 21:26). Thus there is no security to be had. There are two explanations for this. The one offered by Augustine is that at that time some shall be good, but they will be afflicted, they will mourn and they will wait expectantly; and this is referred to in the quotation as "fainting" because of the absence of pleasures and the multiplicity of evils. But there will be peace and security among the evil people. The other explanation is found in the Gloss.

Then when he says, *then sudden destruction will come upon them,* he presents four aspects of the peril. First, that it will be unexpected, where he says: *sudden,* "like a break in a high wall, . . . whose crash comes suddenly, in an instant" (Is. 30:13). Secondly, he describes the peril as bringing death when he says *destruction.* [Destruction will tread upon him as a King" (Job 18:14)]. Thirdly, he refers to the peril as distressing, and he uses the word *travail:* "Anguish as of a woman in travail" (Ps. 48:6). Fourthly, he presents the peril as inevitable when he comments: *and there will be no escape.* Now is the time to escape from the wrath of God to the mercy of God, for the end of the world will not be a time of mercy but of justice.

Then Paul says, *but you are not in darkness, brethren,* and explains what he had mentioned in regard to the good people; and he does this by making two points: first, he excludes the good people from the company of the evil people and secondly, he provides a reason for this (5:5). And so he remarks, *you are not in darkness,* for you have been enlightened by Christ concerning that day; this is not an unexpected event for you. "He who follows me will not walk in darkness, but will have the light of life" (Jn. 8:12). And the reason for this is given at the words: *for you are all sons of light.* He also makes the point that they are the sons of the light *and of the day.* According to the Scriptures, someone is said to be the son of something because he abounds in that thing. "My beloved had a vineyard on a [hill, the son of oil, i.e., a] very fertile hill" (Is. 5:1), that is, it was land which was very rich. Those who participate to a great extent in the day and in the light are called their sons. And this light is the faith of Christ. "I am the light of the world" (Jn. 8:12), and again: "Believe in the light, that you may become sons of light" (Jn. 12:36).

In addition he says, *of the day,* for just as out of the early light comes the fullness of the day, so out of the faith of Christ comes the day which is the brilliance of good actions. "The night is far gone, the day is at hand" (Rom. 13:12). And because of this, you are not sons *of the night,* that is, involved in infidelity; *or of darkness,* that is, of sins. "Let us then cast off the works of darkness and put on the armor of light" (Rom. 13:12).

Then when he says: *so then, let us not sleep,* he shows them how they should prepare themselves for that coming. First, they should prepare themselves for it by keeping away from anything evil; secondly, they should prepare themselves by regularly doing something virtuous (5:8).

In making the first point he does two things. First, he provides a warning, and next he sets down the reason for the warning (5:7). Paul says, therefore, that for this reason the day of the Lord is like a thief: "If the householder had known

at what hour the thief was coming, he would have been awake"
(Lk. 12:39). And so you know you ought to be vigilant. He
adds: *so then, let us not sleep* in the sleep of sin: "Awake, O
sleeper, and arise from the dead" (Eph. 5:14). "How long will
you lie there, O sluggard? When will you arise from your
sleep?" (Prov. 6:9).

But let us keep awake out of solicitude. "Watch therefore,
for you do not know on what day your Lord is coming" (Matt.
24:42). And to this end it is necessary that we *be sober* in order
that both the body and the mind be sober, that is, free from
the pleasures and cares of the world. "But take heed to yourselves lest your hearts be weighed down with dissipation and
drunkenness" (Lk. 21:34). "Be sober, be watchful" (1 Pet.
5:8). And the reason for this is the suitability of a certain time;
those who sleep or get drunk do so at night. But the night is
not for us: *so then, let us not sleep, as others do.* And so Paul
says: *for those who sleep, sleep at night,* that is, at night they
get some rest and during the day they are active. "When the
sun rises, they get them away and lie down in their dens" (Ps.
104:32). And again "Man goes forth to his work and to his
labor until the evening" (Ps. 104:23).

There are also some who do not drink during the day because
of the business which must be accomplished; but they are not
so careful at night. "The eye of the adulterer also waits for the
twilight" (Job 24:15). So sleep and drunkenness are suitable
to nighttime, since drunkards are occupied with sin during
the night of unbelief and the darkness of sin without having
any regard for the future because of the love they have for
present concerns. "They have become callous and have given
themselves up to licentiousness, greedy to practice every kind
of uncleanness" (Eph. 4:19). *But, since we belong to the day,*
that is, belong to the daytime of honesty and faith, *let us be
sober.* "Let us conduct ourselves becomingly as in the day"
(Rom. 13:13).

Then when Paul says: *Let us put on the breastplate of faith,*
he shows how they should prepare themselves through good
actions. First, he sets down a general admonition, and then he
issues a special admonition (5:11). He divides the first point

into two aspects; he first sets down the admonition itself and then he gives a reason for it (5:9). There are in man two important parts of the body which were protected in wars—the heart, which is the source of life, and the head, which governs the body's movements and is the seat of the senses and the center of the nervous system. The heart is protected by a breastplate and the head by a helmet. The life of the spirit in us is Christ, through whom the soul lives and the Lord dwells in us: "That Christ may dwell in your hearts through faith, that you, being rooted and grounded in love . . ." (Eph. 3:17). "He who abides in love abides in God, and God abides in him" (1 Jn. 4:16). Love gives life to faith. So we must have faith and love, and so Paul calls for *the breastplate of faith and love,* because it protects the vital parts of the body, *and for a helmet the hope of salvation,* for salvation is a spiritual motive force because it is the goal which we hope to attain.

Then when he says, *for God has not destined us for wrath,* he shows the manner in which God works in us; this is first shown to be out of divine preordination and then as derived from the grace of Christ. Finally, Paul treats the manner in which salvation is to be achieved. He begins with the words, *God has not destined us,* that is, God has not appointed us: "(I) appointed you that you should go and bear fruit" (Jn. 15:16); *for wrath,* that is, that we should deserve His wrath: "God did not make death" (Wis. 1:13). "Have I any pleasure in the death of the wicked, says the Lord God, and not rather that he should turn from his way and live? (Ez. 18:23). *But to obtain salvation,* that is, that we might acquire salvation. "From the days of John the Baptist until now the kingdom of heaven has suffered violence, and men of violence take it by force" (Matt. 11:12). "But you are a chosen race, a royal priesthood, a holy nation, God's own people" (1 Pet. 2:9). And this is achieved through Christ's grace; hence he says, *through our Lord Jesus Christ.* "For there is no other name under heaven given among men by which we must be saved" (Ac. 4:12).

Who died for us, that is, He redeemed us by dying for us. "The righteous (died) for the unrighteous, that he might bring us to God, being put to death in the flesh but made alive in the spirit" (1 Pet. 3:18). And the manner of attaining salvation is also through Him, for Christ taught us this while working for our salvation, which He achieved by dying and rising again. "Who was put to death for our trespasses and raised for our justification" (Rom. 4:25). And so Paul says: *so that whether we wake or sleep, we might live with him.* "Whether we live or whether we die, we are the Lord's (Rom. 14:8).

Then when he says, *therefore encourage one another,* he teaches us how we should behave toward special classes of people. And in this regard he makes three points; first, he shows how they should behave towards their equals; secondly, how they should be subject to their bishop (5:12). And finally, he shows how the bishops should behave toward their flock (5:14).

To our equals we owe consolation in times of difficulty, and so he says, *encourage one another.* In addition, they should inspire them through example, and so he says, *and build one another up.* "Let us then pursue what makes for peace and for mutual upbuilding" (Rom. 14:19).

Those who are subject to bishops owe them, first, the acknowledgement of blessings; secondly, charity; and thirdly, peace. *Respect those who labor among you,* that is, acknowledge their work: "Remember your leaders, those who spoke to you the word of God" (Heb. 13:7). And I say that you shall respect them first on their own behalf, because of the great labours they have borne for you. And so he makes mention of *those who labour among you* for your good. "Take your share of suffering as a good soldier of Christ Jesus" (2 Tim. 2:3). Secondly, you shall respect them on behalf of God, and because of this reverence is due to them as it is due to God. And so Paul remarks: *and are over you in the Lord,* that is, in the place of God. "If I have forgiven anything, it has been for your sake in the presence of Christ" (2 Cor. 2:10). Thirdly, you shall respect them on your own behalf, because they are useful to you; hence he says: *and they admonish you.* Furthermore, you owe them charity; hence, *esteem them very highly in love,* that is, before others.

Finally, *because of their work, be at peace* [with them]. Yet some act against this. "They hate him who reproves in the gate, and they abhor him who speaks the truth" (Am. 5:10). "One who rejoices in wickedness will be condemned" (Sir. 19:5). Nevertheless, you should be at peace with them because of their work of correction, for this work properly belongs to their office. "I am for peace; but when I speak, they are for war" (Ps. 120:7).

5–2

14 And we exhort you, brethren, admonish the idle, encourage the fainthearted, help the weak, be patient with them all. 15 See that none of you repays evil for evil, but always seek to do good to one another and to all. 16 Rejoice always, 17 pray constantly, 18 give thanks in all circumstances; for this is the will of God in Christ Jesus for you. 19 Do not quench the Spirit, 20 do not despise prophesying, 21 but test everything; hold fast what is good, 22 abstain from every form of evil. 23 May the God of peace himself sanctify you wholly; and may your spirit and soul and body be kept sound and blameless at the coming of our Lord Jesus Christ. 24 He who calls you is faithful, and he will do it. 25 Brethren, pray for us. 26 Greet all the brethren with a holy kiss. 27 I adjure you by the Lord that this letter be read to all the brethren. 28 The grace of our Lord Jesus Christ be with you.

Earlier he showed them how they ought to remain subject to their bishops. Here he makes the same point from another point of view. And concerning this he does two things. He first teaches how bishops should act toward their priests, and secondly he teaches them in general how they ought to behave towards everyone (5:15). It should be understood that the concern of bishops should be directed toward two things, that is, to prevent others from sinning and to safeguard themselves in this respect.

In treating the first point, Paul does three things; because there are three ways in which persons subject to authority may fail: first, in action; secondly, in the will; thirdly, in virtue.

They fail in action when they give themselves over to the act of sinning; and then they ought to be corrected. And, although they ought to be corrected concerning every sin, they should be corrected especially with respect to the sin of idleness, and so Paul remarks: *admonish the idle.* "We were not idle when we were with you" (2 Thess. 3:7). "Question your neighbor before you threaten him" (Sir. 19:17).

Their will may be at fault if no great tasks are undertaken because they are despondent as a result of their adversities and their earlier sins. Consequently Paul says, *encourage the fainthearted.* A person is considered fainthearted if he has no courage for great things because he is afraid of failing. "Say to those who are of a fearful heart, Be strong, fear not!" (Is. 35:4). "Your words have upheld him who was stumbling" (Job 4:4).

They fail in virtue, whenever they sin because of weakness or are halfhearted in a good act; and these people need to be encouraged. So Paul remarks, *help,* that is, befriend in all charity, *the weak,* for their power is weak for resisting evil or for doing charitable works. "We who are strong ought to bear with the failings of the weak" (Rom. 15:1).

A bishop ought to guard himself against a fault of any kind, and mainly against impatience, for he is bearing the full burden of the group. "I am not able to carry all this people alone, the burden is too heavy for me" (Num. 11:14). Hence he says, *be patient with them all.* "Good sense makes a man slow to anger" (Prov. 19:11).

Then, when Paul says: *see that none of you repays evil for evil,* he shows them in general how they ought to behave towards everyone. And concerning this, he does two things: first, he shows how everyone should behave in certain matters; secondly, he shows how they should behave in all things (5:21). In regards to the first, he makes three points: first, he shows how they ought to behave towards their fellow men; secondly, how to behave in matters that pertain to God (5:16); thirdly, how to conduct themselves with respect to His gifts (5:19).

They should not be mean to their fellow men but should try to be kind to them. Paul says that earlier I spoke in particular, but now I say this in general: *see that none of you repays evil for evil.* "If I have requited my friend with evil let the enemy pursue me . . ." (Ps. 7:4).

On the other hand, repayment is frequently sought before a judge. I wish to point out that the moral act is specified by the intended end. The intention, however, can be of two kinds, that is, either the mere misfortune of someone may be desired, and this is illicit because of the evil character of revenge: or the act may be aimed at the good of correction or of that of justice and the protection of the public interest. And, in this case, it does not render evil for evil but rather good, which is the corrective for evil.

Concerning the second point, Paul says, *always seek to do good.* And he says *seek* and not "do," for it is you who must seek opportunity for doing good to your neighbor without waiting for him to supply you with an opportunity for doing good to him. "Seek peace, and pursue it" (Ps. 34:14). "Do not be overcome by evil" (that is, so that you be attracted by it for doing wrong) "but overcome evil with good" (Rom. 12:21). "As we have opportunity, let us do good to all men" (Gal. 6:10).

Then when Paul says: *rejoice always,* he shows how they ought to behave towards God; and he mentions three things. First, to rejoice in Him; and so Paul says, *rejoice always,* that is, in God; for whatever evil might occur, it is incomparable to the goodness which is God. Hence, no evil ought to interrupt it, and so Paul insists: *rejoice always.* Secondly, to pray for the blessings they want to receive. Paul urges, *pray constantly.* "They ought always to pray and not lose heart" (Lk. 18:1).

How is this possible? It may happen in three ways. First, that person who does not neglect the appointed hours for prayer, prays always. "You shall eat at my table always" (2 Sam. 9:7). Secondly, "pray constantly" means to pray continuously. But then prayer is considered under the aspect of the effect of the prayer. For prayer is the unfolding or expression of desire; for when I desire something, then I ask for it by praying. So prayer is the petition of suitable things from God; and so desire has the power of prayer. "O Lord, thou wilt hear the desire of the meek" (Ps. 10:17). Therefore, whatever we do is the result of a desire; so prayer always remains in force in the good things we do; for the good things we do flow forth from the desire of the good. There is a commentary on this verse pointing out: "He does not cease praying, who does not cease doing good." A third way by which it is possible to pray without ceasing is through the giving of alms which may be a sort of cause of continual prayer. In the lives of the Fathers we read: "He who gives alms is the one who always prays, for the person who receives alms prays for you even when you are asleep."

The third thing he mentions is to offer thanks for those blessings already received, hence Paul says: *in all circumstances,* that is, in good times and in bad times, *give thanks.* "We know that in everything God works for good with those who love him" (Rom. 6:28). "Abounding in thanksgiving" (Col. 2:7). "With thanksgiving" (Phil. 4:6). *For this is the will of God in Christ Jesus for you.* "Who desires all men to be saved and to come to the knowledge of the truth" (1 Tim. 2:4).

Then when he says, *do not quench the Spirit,* he shows them how they are to regard the gifts of God. First, Paul shows that they must not curtail them; secondly, that they must not have a disdain for the gifts of God (5:20). The Holy Spirit is a divine, incorruptible and eternal person; and so He cannot be extinguished in His own substance. Nevertheless someone is said to quench the Spirit, in one way, by extinguishing the ardor for the Spirit either in himself or in somebody else. "Be aglow with the Spirit" (Rom. 12:11). For when somebody wishes to do something generous as a result of the impulse of the Holy Spirit, or even when some generous inclination arises, and the person impedes it, he extinguishes the Holy Spirit. "You always resist the Holy Spirit" (Ac. 7:51).

In another way one may extinguish the Holy Spirit by mortal sin. For the Holy Spirit always abides in Himself; but He abides in us when He makes us abide in Him. But when somebody commits a mortal sin, the Holy Spirit does not abide in him. "For a holy and disciplined spirit will flee from deceit, and will rise and depart from foolish thoughts, and will be ashamed at the approach of unrighteousness" (Wis. 1:5).

A third way in which one may extinguish the Spirit is by

concealing Him; this is meant to imply that if you have the gift of the Spirit, make use of it for the benefit of your neighbors. "Hidden wisdom and unseen treasure, what advantage is there in either of them? (Sir. 20:30). "Nor do men light a lamp and put it under a bushel, but on a stand, and it gives light to all in the house" (Matt. 5:15).

Do not despise prophesying. For some among these people were gifted with prophecies but were considered insane by them. "Earnestly desire the spiritual gifts, especially that you may prophesy" (1 Cor. 14:1). Or else *prophesying* may be understood as divine doctrine; for those who explain divine doctrine are called prophets. In this case, do not despise the words of God and preachers. "For the word of the Lord has become for me a reproach and derision all day long" (Jer. 20:8).

Then when he says, *but test everything,* he shows how they ought to behave towards everything; and one piece of advice is that they should make use of discretion in all matters. "Your spiritual worship" ["Your reasonable service"] (Rom. 12:1). In this matter there should be a careful examination, the election of the good, and the rejection of the evil.

In treating the first point Paul says, *do not despise prophesying,* nevertheless, *test everything,* that is, those which are dubious; for matters that are evident do not require examination. "Do not believe every spirit" (1 Jn. 4:1). "Does not the ear try words?" (Job 12:11). Concerning the second, he says, *hold fast what is good.* "For a good purpose it is always good to be made much of" (Gal. 4:18). In regard to the third point, Paul says of evil: *abstain from every form of evil.* "He knows how to refuse the evil and choose the good" (Is. 7:15). And he says, *every form* because we are obliged to avoid even those actions which only have the appearance of evil, that is, which we cannot perform in the sight of men without causing scandal.

Then, when Paul says: *may the God of peace himself sanctify you wholly,* he interjects a prayer; and he does three things. First, he prays on their behalf; secondly, he indicates that his prayer will be heard; and finally he issues special admonitions. Paul says, I have given my advice; but remember that nothing will come of it unless God gives you grace. There-fore, *may the God of peace himself sanctify you.* "I am the Lord who sanctify you" (Lev. 22:32). *Wholly,* that you may be totally holy, and this in order that *your spirit and soul and body be kept sound.*

On account of these words, certain people maintained that the spirit in man is one element and the soul another, thus positing two souls in man, that is, one which animates the body and another which carries on the function of reasoning. These opinions are rejected in the Church's teaching. For it should be realized that these two elements [which are really one] do not differ essentially, but only by reason of the powers present in them. There are certain powers in our soul which are linked to bodily organs, such as the powers of the sensitive part of the soul. And there are other powers which are not linked to bodily organs, but function apart from the body, insofar as they are the powers of the intellectual part of the soul. The latter powers are regarded as spiritual powers in that they are immaterial and separated in some manner from the body in that they are not functions of the body but are referred to as the mind. "Be renewed in the spirit of your minds" (Eph. 4:23). Yet it is called the soul insofar as it animates the body, for this is proper to it. Paul speaks here in a specific sense.

Now there are three elements involved in sin: reason, the sensitive appetite, and the actual actions of the body. Paul is anxious that all three of these areas be free of sin. Since he wants reason to be free of sin, he says: *may your spirit,* that is, your mind, *be kept sound.* For in every sin, reason is corrupted in the sense that every bad person is in some way ignorant. There should be no sin in the sensitive appetite either, and Paul refers to this when he says: *and soul.* Nor should there be sin in the body, and so Paul adds: *and body.* This, however, is achieved when the body is preserved immune from sin.

Paul also says: *and blameless,* instead of "not without sin" which may be attributed only to Christ; but to be "blameless" may also be said of those who, although they may commit venial sins, nevertheless have not committed grave sins by which their fellow men may be scandalized. "Walking in all the commandments and ordinances of the Lord blameless" (Lk. 1:6). And Paul adds, *at the coming of our Lord Jesus Christ,* that is, persevering until the end of life. Or, perhaps the word *spirit* may refer to the gift of the Holy Spirit, as if implying: may the gift of the Holy Spirit which you have be unimpaired.

Then when Paul says: *He who calls you is faithful,* he expresses the hope that his prayer will be heard, as if saying: it will come about as I hope, for He who calls you *will do it,* that is, He will accomplish it. "The Lord is faithful in all his words" (Ps. 145:13). "And those whom he called he also justified" (Rom. 8:30).

Finally, Paul adds certain familiar admonitions as when he urges prayer: *pray;* and mutual peace: *greet all the brethren with a holy kiss,* not a treacherous kiss as that of Judas (Matt. 26), nor a passionate kiss like that of the lustful woman in Proverbs (7:13).

I adjure you by the Lord that this letter be read to all the brethren. Paul feared that those in charge of the assembly might suppress it because of some of the things contained in it. "The people curse him who holds back grain, but a blessing is on the head of him who sells it" (Prov. 11:26).

Finally, he concludes the letter with a salutation.

LETTER TO THE PHILIPPIANS

TRANSLATED BY F. R. LARCHER, O.P.

Philippi was another important city in Macedonia. It was named after Philip of Macedon, and evangelized by St. Paul during his second missionary journey. In fact, the church at Philippi was the first to be founded by Paul in Europe and he always enjoyed very personal and warm relations with the Christian Philippians. Details of its founding are found in Acts (16:11–40).

The occasion of this letter was that the church at Philippi had heard that Paul had been cast into prison. In order to assist him, it sent Epaphroditus with a sum of money to do whatever he could. While helping Paul, Epaphroditus fell seriously ill and almost died. Upon his recovery Paul decided to send him back to Philippi.

This letter thanks the Philippians for their help and concern and contains many valuable counsels. Very notable is the "poem of the humility of the Messiah" (2:6–11), showing the belief of the early Church in the divine pre-existence of Jesus.

It is not certain when this letter was written. The customary alternatives proposed are from Rome about 63, or from Ephesus about 56–57.

For the characteristics of St. Thomas' exegesis see the *Introduction* of Matthew L. Lamb to his translation of the letter to the Ephesians in this same series.

PROLOGUE

The path of the righteous is like the light of dawn, which shines brighter and brighter until full day (Prov. 4:18).

In this text the life of the saints is described under three aspects: first, its narrowness, when it is called a *path:* "For the gate is narrow and the way is hard, that leads to life" (Mt. 7:14); "That path no bird of prey knows, and the falcon's eye has not seen it" (Job 28:7); secondly, its splendor when he says, *the light of dawn:* "For once you were darkness, but now you are light in the Lord" (Eph. 5:8). For the just shine and, as a result, their life shines. Thirdly, its progress, because it is always growing: "Long for the pure spiritual milk, that by it you may grow up to salvation" (1 Pet. 2:2); and this even until the *full day* of glory; "When the perfect comes, the imperfect will pass away" (1 Cor. 13:10).

The way of the wicked, on the other hand, is wide, obscure, dark and failing: "The way of the wicked is like deep darkness: they do not know over what they stumble" (Prov. 4:19); "The gate is wide and the way is easy, that leads to destruction, and those who enter by it are many" (Mt. 7:13).

From these words we can gather the subject matter of this letter. For the Philippians were on Christ's narrow way, enduring many tribulations for Christ. They were enlightened by faith: "Among whom you shine as lights in the world" (Phil. 2:15). Furthermore, they were making progress, as is clear from the entire letter. Therefore, after the letter to the Ephesians, in which an instruction was given on preserving Church

57

unity, it was fitting that those who best preserved it should be held up as an example of preserving the unity of the Church.

1–1

1 Paul and Timothy, servants of Christ Jesus, to all the saints in Christ Jesus who are at Philippi, with the bishops and deacons: 2 Grace to you and peace from God our Father and the Lord Jesus Christ. 3 I thank my God in all my remembrance of you, 4 always in every prayer of mine for you all making my prayer with joy, 5 thankful for your partnership in the gospel from the first day until now. 6 And I am sure that he who began a good work in you will bring it to completion at the day of Jesus Christ. 7 It is right for me to feel thus about you all, because I hold you in my heart, for you are all partakers with me of grace, both in my imprisonment and in the defense and confirmation of the gospel.

This letter is divided into a greeting and a message (1:3). In the greeting he does three things: first, the persons who send the greeting are described; secondly, the persons greeted (1:1); thirdly, the good things he wishes them (1:2). In regard to the first he does two things: first, he mentions the persons who send the greeting; secondly, their condition (1:1).

In regard to the first he mentions, first of all, the principal person, when he says, *Paul,* which means "small." In this he indicates his humility: "The least one shall become a clan, and the smallest one a mighty nation" (Is. 60:22). Secondly, the co-sender, when he says, *and Timothy,* because he was their preacher: "I have no one like him, who will be genuinely anxious for your welfare" (*infra* 2:20).

Then when he says, *servants of Christ Jesus,* he states their condition: "For what we preach is not ourselves, but Jesus Christ as Lord, with ourselves as your servants for Jesus' sake" (2 Cor. 4:5). But this seems to conflict with John (15:15): "No longer do I call you servants, for the servant does not know what his master is doing." I answer that there are two kinds of servitude, corresponding to the two kinds of fear. Fear of punishment causes evil servitude, and this is the kind meant in the above text from John. But chaste fear causes reverential servitude, which is the kind the Apostle has in mind.

The persons greeted are the saints of the Church in Philippi: first, the lesser ones; hence he says, *to all the saints who are at Philippi,* which is a city founded by Philip. He calls them *saints* on account of their baptism: "Do you not know that all of us who have been baptized into Christ Jesus were baptized into his death?" (Rom. 6:3). He includes the greater ones when he says, *with the bishops and deacons.* But why does he mention the lesser ones before the greater? Because the people are prior to the prelate: "Should not shepherds feed the sheep?" (Ez. 34:2). For the flocks are to be fed by the shepherds, and not vice versa. But why does he not mention the priests? I answer that they are included with the bishops, because there are not a number of bishops in a city; hence when he puts it in the plural, he means to include priests. Yet it is a distinct order, because we read in the gospel that after appointing twelve apostles (whose persons the bishops manifest), He appointed seventy-two disciples, whose place the priests hold. Dionysius also distinguished bishops from priests. But in the beginning, although the orders were distinct, there were not distinct names for the orders; hence here he includes priests with bishops.

Then he mentions the good things he desires for them when he says, *grace to you and peace.* These two goods include everything: first, there is God's *grace* remitting sins: "For by grace you have been saved through faith" (Eph. 2:8); lastly, there is man's *peace:* "He makes peace in your borders" (Ps. 147:14). Consequently, he wishes them all the good things between the two: and this, *from God our Father:* "Every good endowment and every perfect gift is from above, coming down from the Father of lights" (Jas. 1:17), and by the merit of Christ's humanity; hence he says, *and from the Lord Jesus Christ:* "Grace and truth came through Jesus Christ" (Jn. 1:17); "For he is our peace, who has made us both one" (Eph. 2:14).

Then he begins the letter's message, in which he does two

things: first, he gives thanks for past benefits; secondly, he urges them to continue making progress (1:12). In regard to the first: first, he gives thanks for them; secondly, he mentions the subject matter (1:5).

First, therefore, he expresses thanks along with joy and a prayer. And so, touching these three things he says, *I thank my God.* To give thanks is to acknowledge a favor conferred on oneself: "Give thanks in all circumstances" (1 Thess. 5:18). *In all my remembrance of you,* because in regard to them nothing occurred to the Apostle that was not worthy of thanksgiving; and this is very great: "The memory of the righteous is a blessing" (Prov. 10:7). *For you all:* "Your people shall all be righteous; they shall possess the land forever" (Is. 60:21). He gives thanks for their blessings, he makes a *prayer* for their protection, and all of this *with joy:* "Far be it from me that I should sin against the Lord by ceasing to pray for you" (1 Sam. 12:23).

Then when he says, *for your partnership in the gospel,* he touches on the matter of the three things mentioned above. First, he mentions the reason for his thanksgiving; secondly, for his joy in things to come (1:6); thirdly, for his prayer (1:8).

He says, therefore, *for your partnership,* whereby you share in the doctrine of the gospel by believing and by fulfilling it in work; for this is true partnership: "Do not neglect to do good and to share what you have" (Heb. 13:16); *from the first day until now:* "Among thoughtful people stay on" (Si. 27:12). And being confident of this very thing, I take joy in you because, *he who began a good work in you will bring it to completion:* "Cursed is the man who trusts in man" (Jer. 17:5), and in (17:7): "Blessed is the man who trusts in the Lord, whose trust is the Lord." And this by God's power; hence he says, *he who began a good work in you will bring it to completion:* "Apart from me you can do nothing" (Jn. 15:5). This is against the Pelagians, who say that the principle of every good work is from ourselves, but its completion is from God. But this is not true, because the principle in us of every good work is to think of it, and this itself is from God: "Not that we are sufficient of ourselves to claim anything as coming from us; our sufficiency is from God" (2 Cor. 3:5). *At the day of Jesus Christ,* when He will reward each person: "Henceforth there is laid up for me the crown of righteousness, which the Lord, the righteous judge, will award to me on that day" (2 Tim. 4:8); "He will sustain you to the end, guiltless in the day of our Lord Jesus Christ" (1 Cor. 1:8).

The reason for his joy is given when he says: *It is right for me to feel thus about you all,* because it is right that you should rejoice with me in my blessing, *because I hold you in my heart.* As if to say: I have this knowledge of you that you are such; therefore, I rejoice so that you might rejoice in the things in which I rejoice, which is *in my imprisonment.* For he was imprisoned for Christ at that time and he rejoiced in it: "Count it all joy, my brethren, when you meet various trials, for you know that the testing of your faith produces steadfastness. And let steadfastness have its full effect" (Jas. 1:2); "Then they left the presence of the council, rejoicing that they were counted worthy to suffer dishonor for the name" (Acts 5:41). *And in the defense and confirmation of the gospel,* namely, in preaching boldly against tyrants and heretics, and confirming the gospel in the hearts of the faithful: "He departed and went from place to place through the region of Galatia and Phrygia, strengthening all the disciples" (Acts 18:23). Or another way according to a Gloss: *in my heart,* i.e., in my desire that you be partakers of eternal joy: "No one will take your joy from you" (Jn. 16:22). And this cannot be snatched from my heart, for even though I am imprisoned and intent on confirming and defending the gospel, my anxiety for you has not slipped from my heart.

1–2

8 For God is my witness, how I yearn for you all with the affection of Christ Jesus. 9 And it is my prayer that your love may abound more and more, with knowledge and all discernment, 10 so that you may approve what is excellent, and may be pure and blameless for the day of Christ, 11 filled with the

fruits of righteousness which come through Jesus Christ, to the
glory and praise of God. 12 I want you to know, brethren, that
what has happened to me has really served to advance the
gospel, 13 so that it has become known throughout the whole
praetorian guard and to all the rest that my imprisonment is
for Christ; 14 and most of the brethren have been made confident in the Lord because of my imprisonment, and are much
more bold to speak the word of God without fear. 15 Some
indeed preach Christ from envy and rivalry, but others from
good will. 16 The latter do it out of love, knowing that I am
put here for the defense of the gospel; 17 the former proclaim
Christ out of partisanship, not sincerely but thinking to afflict
me in my imprisonment.

Having stated the reason for hope concerning the future, he
now indicates the matters for which he makes supplication for
them. First, he mentions his desire, which is shown to be very
fervent; secondly, the matter of his prayer (1:9).

Since the heart's desire is known to God alone, he calls on
God to witness that he prays for them with desire: "Behold,
my witness," God, "is in heaven" (Job 16:19). *How I yearn for
you all*, i.e., I, living *with the affection of Christ Jesus*. Or, how
I long for you to be in it; as if to say: How I long after your
salvation and participation in the merciful heart of Christ.
"Through the tender mercy of our God" (Lk. 1:78): As if to
say that the power of love reaches to the inmost depths of the
heart. Or, I long for you to be in the heart of Jesus Christ, i.e.,
that you may love Him intimately, and that you may be loved
by Him; for man's life consists in this.

Then when he says, *and it is my prayer*, he mentions his
prayer. He asks three things: the first pertains to increasing
charity within. For the interior affections are perfected by
charity; therefore, if one lacks charity, he should desire to
obtain it; if he has it, he should desire that it be made perfect.
Hence he says, *that your love may abound more and more*. God
is the one from whom an increase of charity should be sought,
because God is the only one who works this in us: "God is able
to provide you with every blessing in abundance, so that you

may always have enough of everything and may provide in abundance for every good work" (2 Cor. 9:8). Hence it is necessary that we pray for it, because "unless your righteousness exceeds that of the scribes and Pharisees, you will never enter the kingdom of heaven" (Mt. 5:20).

The second request regards understanding; hence he says, *with knowledge*. But does knowledge arise from charity? It seems so, because it is stated in 1 John (2:27): "But the anointing which you received from him abides in you, and you have no need that any one should teach you; as his anointing teaches you about everything, and is true, and is no lie." Furthermore, charity is the Spirit, of whom it is said in John (16:13): "When the Spirit of truth comes, he will guide you into all the truth." The reason for this is that when a person has a habit, if that habit is right, then right judgment of things pertaining to that habit follows from it; but if it is corrupted, then false judgment follows. Thus, the temperate person has good judgment in regard to sex, but an intemperate person does not, having a false judgment. Now all things that are done by us must be informed with charity. Therefore, a person with charity has a correct judgment both in regard to things knowable; hence he says, *with knowledge*, by which one recognizes the truth and adheres to the truths of faith; and this is the knowledge of holy things mentioned in Wisdom (10:10); and in regard to things to be done; hence he says, *and all discernment* (*sense*), which is the faculty that deals with external objects. Its function is to judge correctly and quickly about the proper object of sense. As a result, this name has been transferred to the internal judgment of reason; hence, those who possess correct judgment in regard to what they should do are called sensible: "Think," i.e., "sense, of the Lord with uprightness" (Wis. 1:1): "To fix one's thought on," i.e., to sense, "her is perfect understanding" (Wis. 6:15). But this discernment should be able not only to recognize, but also to distinguish between, good and evil, and between good and better; hence he says, *so that you may approve what is excellent*: "Earnestly desire the higher gifts" (1 Cor. 12:31) and in (15:1): "Make love your aim, and earnestly desire the spiritual gifts;" hence he says, *what is excellent*.

The third request concerns behavior. First, he mentions immunity from evil, when he says that you may be *pure*. For there are two evils to be avoided: first, internal destruction, by which a man is destroyed in himself; and this is excluded by sincerity: "the unleavened bread of sincerity and truth" (1 Cor. 5:8). The other concerns our neighbor, namely, offenses; hence he says, *and blameless:* "Give no offense to Jews or to Greeks or to the church of God, just as I try to please all men in everything I do" (1 Cor. 10:32); "We put no obstacle in anyone's way, so that no fault may be found with our ministry" (2 Cor. 6:3). *For the day of Christ,* i.e., to the end of our lives: "He who endures to the end will be saved" (Mt. 24:13). As to the effects of grace he says, *filled with the fruits of righteousness.* Good works are the fruit: "The return (fruit) you get is sanctification and its end, eternal life" (Rom. 6:22). Or, *the fruits of righteousness,* i.e., the reward of justice, namely, the crown: "Henceforth there is laid up for me the crown of righteousness" (2 Tim. 4:8); "For the fruit of good labors is renowned" (Wis. 3:15). This is obtained *through Jesus Christ,* because all that we do is good through Him. "Apart from me you can do nothing" (Jn. 15:5). Furthermore, these things must be done for this end, *to the glory and praise of God,* because God is glorified by the works of the saints, since they cause other people to break out in praise of God: "Praise God in his sanctuary (saints)" (Ps. 150:1); "And it shall be to me a name of joy, a praise and a glory before all the nations of the earth who shall hear of all the good that I do for them" (Jer. 33:9).

Then when he says, *I want you to know, brethren,* he advises them in regard to the future. First, he gives examples to be followed and to be avoided; secondly, he concludes his moral exhortation (ch. 4). In regard to the first he does two things: first, he shows what should be imitated; secondly, what should be avoided (ch. 3). The first is divided into two parts: first, he urges them to imitate him; secondly, to imitate others (ch. 2). The first part is divided into three parts: first, he gives his own progress as an example; secondly, the joy he has in this progress (1:18); thirdly, the fruit of this progress (1:19). The first is again divided into two parts: first, he mentions his progress; secondly, the manner (1:13).

He says, therefore: I have urged you to make progress; and in order that you might have my progress as a pattern, *I want you to know, brethren, that what has happened to me* outwardly, namely, tribulations, did not change me inwardly, but *has really served to advance the gospel,* because the result was that the faith I preached made greater progress: "If we are afflicted, it is for your comfort and salvation; and if we are comforted, it is for your comfort, which you experience when you patiently endure the same sufferings that we suffer" (2 Cor. 1:6).

Then he shows his own progress; secondly, that of others (1:14). In regard to himself, of course, it was obvious that he suffered for Christ with constancy, *so that it has become known . . . that my imprisonment is for Christ.* This redounds to Christ's glory: "But let none of you suffer as a murderer, or a thief, or a wrongdoer, or a mischief-maker; yet if one suffers as a Christian, let him not be ashamed, but under that name let him glorify God" (1 Pet. 4:15). *Throughout the whole praetorian guard,* and in Caesar's court. As for the progress of others, their faith has grown apace: *most of the brethren have been made confident in the Lord because of my imprisonment, and are much more bold to speak the word of God without fear.* "Like the magistrate of the people, so are his officials" (Si. 10:2); "The righteous are bold as a lion" (Prov. 28:1). Yet there is some diversity among these, because some spoke properly and some not. Of those who spoke properly, some did so out of general love, and others out of love for the Apostle; of those who spoke improperly, some acted out of general malice, and some out of personal hatred of the Apostle. Yet it seems to me that the Apostle is revealing the two reasons why some preached: first, because of envy; consequently, to show their evil intention the Apostle says, *from envy and rivalry:* "For where jealousy and selfish ambition exists, there will be disorder and every vile practice" (Jas. 3:16); "For while there is jealousy and strife among you, are you not of the flesh?" (1 Cor. 3:5);

secondly, out of love for Christ and the gospel; hence he says, *but others from good will:* "Deal favorably, O Lord, in your good will with Sion" (Ps. 50:20). The Apostle continues, *the latter do it out of love,* which causes good will, because they preached to make up for my being prevented from teaching. Then the Apostle explains what he had said, saying that, *the former proclaim Christ out of partisanship* and not according to a right intention. For their depraved intention is clear in two ways: first, by preaching publicly they caused a disturbance among the Gentiles against the Apostle and thus added to the affliction he already had; secondly, because they believed that Paul would be disturbed, when he heard that they were usurping the task committed to him, thereby adding more affliction to one already afflicted.

1–3

18 What then? Only that in every way, whether in pretense or in truth, Christ is proclaimed; and in that I rejoice. 19 Yes, and I shall rejoice. For I know that through your prayers and the help of the Spirit of Jesus Christ this will turn out for my deliverance, 20 as it is my eager expectation and hope that I shall not be at all ashamed, but that with full courage now as always Christ will be honored in my body, whether by life or by death. 21 For to me to live is Christ, and to die is gain. 22 If it is to be life in the flesh, that means fruitful labor for me. Yet which I shall choose I cannot tell. 23 I am hard pressed between the two. My desire is to depart and be with Christ, for that is far better. 24 But to remain in the flesh is more necessary on your account.

Above, the Apostle described the progress he has made; here he deals with the joy born of this progress: first, the cause of this joy; secondly, the joy itself (1:18b).

Sometimes it happens that joy arises from a good cause, and this directly and of itself; sometimes from an evil cause, and this indirectly and by accident. For when it springs from a good cause, one should rejoice both in the effect and in the cause, as in the case of giving an alms for the glory of God; but when it springs from an evil cause, one should rejoice in the effect but not in the cause, as in the redemption by Christ, since it came about from the crime committed by Judas and the Jews. The same thing happens in the Church when something beneficial results from good preachers with a good intention, and from evil preachers with an evil intention; nevertheless, one should rejoice in both cases, as has been said. He says, therefore: *what then? Only that in every way, whether in pretence or in truth, Christ is proclaimed; and in that I rejoice. Yes, and I shall rejoice.* One announces Christ *in pretense* when he does not chiefly aim at this but at something else, as profit or glory; "He who is estranged seeks pretexts" (Prov. 18:1); but *in truth,* when it is done with a right intention: "Remember now, O Lord, I beseech thee, how I have walked before thee in faithfulness and with a whole heart, and have done what is good in thy sight" (Is. 38:3). But either way the results are good for the Church; hence he says, *Christ is proclaimed, and in that I rejoice,* because if something other than Christ were proclaimed, there would be reason for concern. This happens when false doctrine is taught; "The shepherd who teaches for the sake of the truth should be loved; the hireling who teaches for gain should be tolerated; but the one who teaches what is false must be expelled" (Augustine).

Then he mentions the joy which followed, when he says, *in that,* namely, that my chains are manifested for the sake of Christ, *I rejoice,* at present in the fact that Christ is preached: "If you loved me, you would have rejoiced" (Jn. 14:28); *and I shall rejoice* in the future: "They shall obtain joy and gladness" (Is. 51:11).

Then when he says, *for I know that through your prayers . . . ,* he mentions the fruit resulting from his progress: first, he mentions the fruit; secondly, he raises a question (1:22). In regard to the first he does three things: first, he mentions the fruit; secondly, his help in obtaining it (1:19); thirdly, he assigns the material of the fruit (1:20b).

He says, therefore: I rejoice in these things on account of the fruit resulting from them for life everlasting: "Israel is saved by the Lord with everlasting salvation" (Is. 45:17), because when we do good by helping in the salvation of others, it redounds to our salvation. For if it is true that "whoever causes one of these little ones who believe in me to sin, it would be better for him to have a great millstone fastened about his neck and to be drowned in the depth of the sea" (Mt. 18:6), how much glory does he deserve who gains the salvation of many? Now help depends on three things: first, on prayer by others; hence he says, *through your prayers,* by which I hope to be helped by God: "Pray for one another that you may be healed. The prayer of a righteous man has great power in its effects" (Jas. 5:16). Secondly, on God, in whom we place our hope for salvation: ["In your presence we have conceived, and have been as it were in labor and have brought forth the spirit of salvation"] (Is. 12:18); hence he says, *and the help of the Spirit of Jesus Christ:* "The Spirit helps us in our weakness" (Rom. 8:26). *This will turn out for my deliverance.* He speaks in a simile; for when a person is infirm, he needs to be delivered from his infirmity, if he is to be kept alive; and this is to help. But we are weak and infirm; therefore, we need the help of the Spirit: "He will teach you all things, and bring to your remembrance all that I have said to you" (Jn. 14:26), by helping us, as it were. Thirdly, help depends on our trust in God, because "he who trusts in his riches will fall" (Prov. 11:28). Therefore, our hope must be in God: "Those who trust in the Lord are like Mount Zion, which cannot be moved, but abides forever" (Ps. 125:1); hence he says, *it is my eager expectation and hope.*

But isn't hope the expectation of future happiness? I answer that hope is a movement of the appetite toward an arduous good; and this can occur in two ways: sometimes a person hopes to obtain something by himself, and then there is hope without expectation; but sometimes he hopes to obtain something through someone else, and then there is hope with expectation. This is the way we expect, when we have the hope of obtaining something through someone else: ["With expectation I have

waited for the Lord, and he was attentive to me"] (Ps. 40:1);
"For in this hope we were saved" (Rom. 8:24).

But he says *I know,* and then speaks of *expectation and hope.*
Is this hope certain? The Apostle answers that it is, saying, *I
shall not be at all ashamed:* "None who put their trust in him
will lack strength" (1 Mach. 2:61); "Hope does not disappoint
us" (Rom. 5:5); "Whoever trusted in the Lord and was put to
shame?" (Si. 2:10).

He gives the reason for this and explains it, when he says,
for to me to live is Christ, and to die is gain. The reason is
based on the fact that he is entirely dedicated to the service
of Christ. As if to say: the reason why this will turn out to my
salvation is that I am totally at the service of Christ. He mentions his confidence when he says that *with full courage now
as always Christ will be honored in my body.* As if to say: many
persecute me, but I put my trust in the Lord: "I will trust, and
will not be afraid" (Is. 12:2). *As always,* i.e., from the beginning of my conversion: "At Damascus he had preached boldly
in the name of Jesus" (Acts 9:27); so *now* also: "I hold fast
my righteousness, and will not let it go" (Job 27:6).

He shows that his intention is right because *Christ will be
honored.* Since He is God, He cannot be honored (increased)
or diminished in Himself, but in us, i.e., in our knowledge. For
a person honors Christ when he increases his knowledge of
Him: "Who can extol him as he is?" (Si. 43:31). And this in
word and deed, when the greatness of His effects shows His
greatness. Among these marvelous effects is justification. But
as long as this lies hidden in a man's heart, Christ is not honored by it, except in that heart, but not in regard to others,
until it breaks out into external visible actions. Hence he says,
in my body. Christ is honored in our body in two ways: in one
way, inasmuch as we dedicate our body to his service by em-
ploying our bodies in his ministry: "Glorify God in your body"
(1 Cor. 6:20); in another way by risking our body for Christ:
"If I deliver my body to be burned" (1 Cor. 13:3). The first is
accomplished by life, the second by death: hence he says,
whether by life, because the body acts only when living, *or by
death:* "If we live, we live to the Lord, and if we die, we die to

the Lord" (Rom. 14:8). This can also refer to spiritual death: "Put to death therefore what is earthly in you" (Col. 3:5).

Then he explains how He will be honored by life and death, saying: *for to me to live is Christ, and to die is gain.* Now life produces activity, for that seems to be at the root of man's life which is the principle of his activity. Hence some call that by which they are roused to activity, their life; as hunters call hunting their life, and friends their friend. So, Christ is our life, because the whole principle of our life and activity is Christ; hence the Apostle says, *for to me to live is Christ,* because Christ alone moved him, *and to die is gain.* Here the Apostle is speaking precisely. For a person regards it a gain when he can improve the imperfect life he has; thus a sick person regards a healthy life a gain. Our life is Christ: "Your life is hid with Christ in God" (Col. 3:3). But here it is imperfect: "While we are at home in the body we are away from the Lord" (2 Cor. 5:6). Therefore, when we die in the body, our life, namely, Christ, with whom we are then present, is perfected in us" ["He gives to his beloved in sleep"] (Ps. 126:2); "The time of my departure has come" (2 Tim. 4:6).

Then when he says, *If it is to be life in the flesh, that means fruitful labor for me,* he raises a doubt in regard to what has been said: first, he states the doubt; secondly, he solves it (1:25). In regard to the first he does two things: first, he states the doubt; secondly, he gives a reason for both sides (1:23).

He says, therefore: *If it is to be life in the flesh, that means fruitful labor for me;* as if to say: If Christ is glorified in my body as long as I am alive, my life in the flesh will bear fruit, i.e., if life brings me as its fruit that Christ is honored, life in the flesh is good and fruitful: "The return [fruit] you get is sanctification and its end, eternal life" (Rom. 6:22). Therefore, if that is the case, *I cannot tell which I shall choose,* whether to die or to live: "For we do not know how to pray as we ought" (Rom. 8:26); "The reasoning of mortals is worthless, and our designs are likely to fail" (Wis. 9:14).

But why do you hesitate? Because *I am hard pressed between the two.* First, he gives a reason for one side; secondly, for the other side. The first reason is that there are two impulses in man, the impulse of nature and that of grace: of nature, not to die: "Not that we would be unclothed, but that we would be further clothed" (2 Cor. 5:5); "And another will carry you where you do not wish to go" (Jn. 21:18); and the impulse of grace, which charity follows, is to love God and neighbor. This impulse to love God moves us to be with God; hence he says, *my desire is to depart,* not absolutely, but *to be with Christ:* "We are of good courage, and we would rather be away from the body and at home with the Lord" (2 Cor. 5:8). This shows the error in the opinion of the Greeks that the souls of the saints are not with Christ immediately after death. The reason why I desire this is that to *be with Christ is far better.* "Whom have I in heaven but thee? And there is nothing upon earth that I desire besides thee" (Ps. 73:25); "For a day in thy courts is better than a thousand elsewhere" (Ps. 84:10). But love of neighbor moves us to desire his betterment; hence he says, *but to remain in the flesh is more necessary on your account,* i.e., my life is necessary for your benefit: "For if we are beside ourselves, it is for God; if we are in our right mind, it is for you" (2 Cor. 5:13). Or another way, *I am hard pressed between the two,* i.e., on two sides: there arises a desire *to depart and be with Christ, for that is far better. But to remain in the flesh is more necessary on your account.* The sense is not changed.

But this does not seem to be subject to doubt; indeed, the Apostle seems to be inclined to the worse side. For the love of God rouses the first desire in us, and the love of neighbor the second. But the first is a greater and better desire. Therefore [Paul has chosen the less perfect]. I answer that the love of God is twofold, namely, concupiscible love, by which a man wills to love God and find his delight in Him; and this is for the man's good. The other is the love of friendship, by which a man prefers the honor of God, even over this delight with which he enjoys God; and this is perfect charity. Hence it is stated in Romans (8:38): "For I am sure that neither death, nor life, nor angels, nor principalities, nor things present, nor things to come, nor powers, nor height, nor depth nor anything else in all creation, will be able to separate us from the love of God in Christ Jesus our Lord." And then he continues in (9:3):

"For I could wish that I myself were accursed and cut off from Christ for the sake of my brethren." He said this to show that he possessed a more perfect charity, as though for the love of God and neighbor he was prepared to lose the delight of seeing God. Therefore, he shows this as something more perfect.

1–4

25 Convinced of this, I know that I shall remain and continue with you all, for your progress and joy in the faith, 26 so that in me you may have ample cause to glory in Christ Jesus, because of my coming to you again. 27 Only let your manner of life be worthy of the gospel of Christ, so that whether I come and see you or am absent, I may hear of you that you stand firm in one spirit, with one mind striving side by side for the faith of the gospel, 28 and not frightened in anything by your opponents. This is a clear omen to them of their destruction, but of your salvation, and that from God. 29 For it has been granted to you that for the sake of Christ you should not only believe in him but also suffer for his sake, 30 engaged in the same conflict which you saw and now hear to be mine.

Having stated the doubt and the reason for both sides, he then resolves it: first, as though choosing one side, he foretells what will be the result of his plan to visit them; secondly, he shows what is required on their part (1:26). In regard to the first he does three things: first, he mentions his coming visit; secondly, he shows its fruit; thirdly, he explains this fruit.

He says, therefore: After saying that to remain in the flesh is necessary for you, because my life is fruitful for you, *I know that I shall remain*, being as it were *convinced of this* in God: "The righteous are bold as a lion" (Prov. 28:1); *I shall remain and continue*, i.e., I shall live and continue to live. But on the other hand he was soon killed by Nero. I answer that this letter was written in the first year of his imprisonment, which was also the first year of Nero's reign. Hence he lived for seven years after this.

With you all, i.e., for the benefit of all of you: "I do not seek my own advantage, but that of many, that they may be saved" (1 Cor. 10:33). And this, *for your progress,* i.e., that through my exhortation you may progress in the faith and rejoice in my life, which you have heard about; but you would rejoice more, if I were present: "I long to see you, that I may impart to you some spiritual gift to strengthen you" (Rom. 1:11).

Then he explains what he had said, saying, *so that in me you may have ample cause to glory,* i.e., if it is granted me to come to you again, it will be in order that joy may abound in you: "Now to him who by the power at work within us is able to do far more abundantly than all that we ask or think, to him be glory in the church" (Eph. 3:20). And this *in Christ Jesus,* because the fact that they rejoiced in him was for the sake of Christ: "I want some benefit from you in the Lord" (Philem. 1:20).

Then when he says, *only let your manner of life be worthy of the gospel of Christ,* he shows what is required on their part. He says that the only thing required of them is that they live worthy of the gospel of Christ, in a manner that conforms to that gospel: "We exhorted each one of you and encouraged you and charged you to lead a life worthy of God, who calls you into his own kingdom and glory" (1 Thess. 2:12); "To lead a life worthy of the Lord, fully pleasing to him" (Col. 1:10). And this is my joy: "No greater joy can I have than this, to hear that my children follow the truth" (3 Jn. 4). Now he specifically desires from them unity and constancy. There are three kinds of unity required of the saints: first, the unity of love; hence he says, *that I may hear,* namely, *that you stand firm in one spirit,* through love: "Eager to maintain the unity of the Spirit in the bond of peace" (Eph. 4:3), and in 1 Corinthians (6:17) "He who is united to the Lord becomes one spirit with him." Secondly, the unity of concord; hence he says, *with one mind,* i.e., have one will and one soul: "Now the company of those who believed were of one heart and soul" (Acts 4:32); ["God makes men of one way to dwell in one house"] (Ps. 67:7). Thirdly, the unity of cooperation; hence he says, *striving side by side for the faith of the gospel,* i.e., one helping the other. This is brought about by what is stated in 1 Kings (25:1) "All Israel assembled and mourned for him," namely, Samuel; "A brother helped is like a strong city" (Prov. 18:19).

Secondly, he expects constancy: *and not frightened in anything by your opponents.* First, he urges them to be brave, because their opponents can do only as much as God allows: "But not a hair of your head will perish" (Lk. 21:18); "Its leaf does not wither" (Ps. 1:3); "Who are you that you are afraid of man who dies, of the son of man who is made like grass?" (Is. 51:12). There are three reasons for this: the first is taken from the fruit of tribulation. He says, therefore: *not frightened,* because there is fruit for you in that persecution which *to them,* i.e., to the persecutors, is a *clear omen of their destruction;* but to you it is a cause *of salvation:* "Whoever would save his life will lose it, and whoever loses his life for my sake will find it" (Mt. 16:25); "He who loves his life loses it" (Jn. 12:25); "I will destroy you, O Israel; who can help you?" (Hos. 13:9). And this *from God,* from whom *it has been granted to you* to endure tribulation patiently.

The second reason is that *you should believe in him:* "For by grace you have been saved through faith" (Eph. 2:8), which is the great and first gift; *but also suffer for his sake,* which is a greater gift, namely, that you should act for Christ as his athlete: "Then they left the presence of the council, rejoicing that they were counted worthy to suffer dishonor for the name" (Acts 5:41). This is useful and honorable; hence you should act bravely.

The third reason is taken from his example, because he deals with them as people who are the first fruits of the faith. Hence he says, *engaged in the same conflict which you saw to be mine,* namely, when among you I was naked and beaten by the Philippians because I freed the girl with the spirit of divination (Acts 16); *and now hear to be mine,* who am in prison.

2-1

1 So if there is any encouragement in Christ, any incentive of love, any participation in the Spirit, any affection and sympathy, 2 complete my joy by being of the same mind, having

the same love, being in full accord and of one mind. 3 Do nothing from selfishness or conceit, but in humility count others better than yourselves. 4 Let each of you look not only to his own interests, but also to the interests of others.

Above, he offered himself as an example of patience and holiness; here he presents others as an example of the same: first, he gives the example of Christ; secondly, the examples of his disciples, whom he promises to send to strengthen them (2:19). In regard to the first he does three things: first, he prefaces his exhortation; secondly, he gives an example (2:5); thirdly, he concludes with the example of Christ (2:12). In regard to the first we must consider: first, the means by which he leads them; secondly, to what he leads them (2:2). In regard to the first he uses four means: first, their devotion to Christ; secondly, their love of neighbor; thirdly, their society; fourthly, their mercy.

He says: *So if there is any encouragement in Christ, any incentive of love, any participation in the Spirit, any affection and sympathy.* These four means which were mentioned all refer to his request: *complete my joy.* The meaning is as though he were saying: I want to be consoled in you. *If there is any encouragement in Christ,* i.e., if you wish to afford me consolation in Christ, *complete my joy:* "To grant to those who mourn in Zion—to give to them a garland instead of ashes, the oil of gladness instead of mourning" (Is. 61:3); "Who comforts us in all our affliction, so that we may be able to comfort those who are in any affliction, with the comfort with which we ourselves are comforted by God" (2 Cor. 1:4). As for fraternal charity he says, *if any incentive of love . . . complete my joy:* "The fruit of the Spirit is love, joy, peace" (Gal. 5:22); "Behold, how good and pleasant it is when brothers dwell in unity" (Ps. 133:1).

As for that special fellowship which prevails among men who share various things, as soldiers share the arms of warfare, he says, *if any participation in the Spirit* between me and you, *complete my joy.* As if to say: I have afforded you much consolation; therefore, if you are my companions, afford the same to me: "Eager to maintain the unity of the Spirit in the bond of peace" (Eph. 4:3); "There is a friend who sticks closer than a brother" (Prov. 18:24). As to their mercy he says, *if any affection and sympathy:* "Put on then, as God's chosen ones, holy and beloved, compassion, kindness . . ." (Col. 3:12).

Then he indicates what he is urging them to do: first, in general, when he says, *complete my joy.* As if to say: I always rejoice in you on account of the good things I have seen and heard of you; but when these multiply, my joy will grow and finally become perfect. Therefore, complete it, by making progress in good. Secondly, in particular, when he urges them to mutual love, whose unity consists in two things: first, in the affections: "Let us not love in word or speech but in deed and in truth" (1 Jn. 3:18), bearing on the object of charity; hence he says, *being of the same mind.* For wisdom in the mind is knowledge of the loftiest causes, because it pertains to wisdom to judge, and no one can do this without knowing the highest cause. Consequently, wisdom is concerned with divine things. Therefore, *being of the same mind.* As if to say: Have the same mind in regard to the things of faith: "May the God of steadfastness and encouragement grant you to live in such harmony with one another, in accord with Christ Jesus, that together you may with one voice glorify the God and Father of our Lord Jesus Christ" (Rom. 15:5). But this depends on having the same charity; hence he says, *having the same love:* "And above all these put on love, which binds everything together in perfect harmony" (Col. 3:14). As for its effect, which consists in two persons consenting to the same thing, two things are required. As to the first he says, *being in full accord,* namely, in acting: ["God makes men of one way to dwell in one house" (Ps. 67:7)]; "That together you may with one voice glorify God" (Rom. 15:6). As to the second he says, *and of one mind.* This differs from the statement *being of the same mind,* as *being in full accord* differs from *having the same love.*

Then he exhorts them to humility: first, he excludes whatever is contrary to humility; secondly, he exhorts them to it. The things contrary to humility are those which spring from pride: one is outward contention, because the humble yield to one another: "By insolence the heedless make strife" (Prov. 13:10);

"For where jealousy and selfish ambition exist, there will be disorder and every vile practice" (Jas. 3:16). Therefore, he says, *do nothing from selfishness*. The other is vainglory, for a proud person desires his own excellence, even in the opinion of others: "Let us have no self-conceit, no provoking of one another, no envy of one another" (Gal. 5:26); "I do not seek my own glory; there is One who seeks it and he will be the judge" (Jn. 8:50). Thus, he says here, *or conceit*. This is followed by the admonition, *but in humility count others better than your-selves*. For just as it pertains to pride that a man extol himself above himself, so to humility that he restrain himself according to his limitations.

But how can a superior person do this? For he either does not know that he is superior and virtuous, and then he is not virtu-ous, because he is not prudent; or he does know, and then he cannot consider some as superior to himself. I answer that no one is so good that there is no defect in him, or so evil that he has no good. Therefore, he should not prefer another to himself absolutely, but because he can say in his mind: "Per-haps there is some defect in me that is not in this other person." Augustine shows this in the book *On Virginity*, when he recom-mends that a virgin prefer a married woman to herself on the ground that she may be more fervent. But suppose that one person is good from every aspect, and another evil; neverthe-less, you and he bear a double person, namely, yours and Christ's. Therefore, if you cannot prefer him to yourself by reason of his person, you can do so by reason of the divine image: "Outdo one another in showing honor" (Rom. 12:10).

Thirdly, he urges them to mutual care, saying *let each of you look not only to his own interests, but also to the interests of others*: "That the members may have the same care for one another" (1 Cor. 12:25); "Love does not insist on its own way" (1 Cor. 13:5).

2–2

5 Have this mind among yourselves, which you have in Christ Jesus, 6 who, though he was in the form of God, did not count

equality with God a thing to be grasped, 7 but emptied himself,
taking the form of a servant, being born in the likeness of men.
8 And being found in human form he humbled himself and
became obedient unto death, even death on a cross.

After giving his exhortation, the Apostle urges them to the
virtue of humility according to Christ's example. First, he exhorts them to follow the example of Christ; secondly, he gives
the example (2:6).

He says, therefore: Be humble, as I have said; hence *have
this mind among yourselves,* i.e., acquire by experience the
mind *which you have in Christ Jesus.* It should be noted that
we should have this mind in five ways according to the five
senses: first, to see His glory, so that being enlightened, we may
be conformed to Him: "Your eyes will see the king in his
beauty" (Is. 33:17); "And we all, with unveiled face, beholding
the glory of the Lord, are being changed into his likeness from
one degree of glory to another" (2 Cor. 3:18); secondly, to
hear His wisdom, in order to become happy: "Happy are these
your servants, who continually stand before you and hear your
wisdom" (1 Kgs. 10:8); "As soon as they heard of me they
obeyed me" (Ps. 18:44). Thirdly, to smell the grace of His
meekness, that we may run to Him: "Your anointing oils are
fragrant . . . draw me after you" (Cant. 1:3); fourthly, to
taste the sweetness of His mercy, that we may always be in
God: "Taste and see that the Lord is good" (Ps. 34:9); fifthly,
to touch His power, that we may be saved: "If I only touch his
garment, I shall be made well" (Mt. 9:21).

Then when he says, *who, though he was in the form of God,*
etc., he proposes the example of Christ. First, he mentions
Christ's majesty; secondly, His humility (2:7); thirdly, His
exaltation (2:9).

He mentions Christ's majesty first, in order that His humility
might be more easily recommended. In regard to His majesty
he proposes two things, namely, the truth of His divine nature,
and His equality. He says, therefore: *who,* namely, Christ,
though he was in the form of God. For it is through its form
that a thing is said to be in a specific or generic nature; hence

the form is called the nature of a thing. Consequently, to be in the form of God is to be in the nature of God. By this is understood that He is true God: ["That we may be in his true Son, Jesus Christ" (1 Jn. 5:20)]. However, it should not be supposed that the form of God is one thing and God himself another, because in simple and immaterial things, and especially in God, the form is the same as that whose form it is.

But why does he say, *in the form*, rather than "in the nature"? Because this belongs to the proper names of the Son in three ways: for He is called the Son, the Word and the Image. Now the Son is the one begotten, and the end of begetting is the form. Therefore, to show the perfect Son of God he says, *in the form*, as though having the form of the Father perfectly. Similarly, a word is not perfect unless it leads to a knowledge of a thing's nature; and so the Word of God is said to be in the form of God, because He has the entire nature of the Father. Finally, an image is not perfect, unless it has the form of that of which it is the image: "He reflects the glory of God and bears the very stamp of his nature" (Heb. 1:3).

But does He have it perfectly? Yes, because He *did not count equality with God a thing to be grasped*. This can be taken two ways: in one way, of His humanity. But this is not the way Paul understood it, because it would be heretical; for it would be a grasping [robbery] if it referred to his humanity. Therefore, it must be explained in another way, namely, of His divinity, according to which equality with God is said of Christ. It is contrary to reason to say otherwise: because the nature of God cannot be received in matter; but the fact that someone existing in a certain nature participates in that nature to a greater or lesser degree is due to the matter; which is not the case here. Therefore, we must say that He *did not count equality with God a thing to be grasped*, because He is in the form of God and knows His own nature well. And because He knows this, it is stated in John (5:18): "He called God his Father, making himself equal with God." But this is not a grasping, as it was when the devil and man wished to be equal to Him: "I will make myself like the Most High" (Is. 14:14); "You will be like God" (Gen. 3:5), for which Christ came to make statisfaction: "What I did not steal must I now restore?" (Ps. 69:4).

Then when he says, *but emptied himself*, he commends Christ's humility: first, as to the mystery of the incarnation; secondly, as to the mystery of the passion (2:8). In regard to the first: first, he mentions His humility; secondly, its manner and form (2:7).

He says, therefore, He *emptied himself*. But since He was filled with the divinity, did He empty Himself of that? No, because He remained what He was; and what He was not, He assumed. But this must be understood in regard to the assumption of what He had not, and not according to the assumption of what He had. For just as He descended from heaven, not that He ceased to exist in heaven, but because He began to exist in a new way on earth, so He also emptied Himself, not by putting off His divine nature, but by assuming a human nature.

How beautiful to say that He *emptied himself*, for the empty is opposed to the full! For the divine nature is sufficiently full, because every perfection of goodness is there. But human nature and the soul are not full, but capable of fulness, because it was made as a slate not written upon. Therefore, human nature is empty. Hence he says, He *emptied himself*, because He assumed a human nature.

First, he touches on the assumption of human nature when he says, *taking the form of a servant*. For by reason of his creation man is a servant, and human nature is the form of a servant: "Know that the Lord is God! It is he that made us, and we are his" (Ps. 100:3); "Behold my servant, whom I uphold" (Is. 42:1); "But thou, O, Lord, art a shield about me" (Ps. 3:4). But why is it more fitting to say *the form of a servant*, rather than "servant"? Because servant is the name of a hypostasis, which was not assumed, but the nature was; for that which is assumed is distinct from the one assuming it. Therefore, the Son of God did not assume a man, because that would mean that he was other than the Son of God; nevertheless, the Son of God became man. Therefore, He took the nature to His own person, so that the Son of God and the Son of man would be the same in person.

Secondly, he touches on the conformity of His nature to ours when he says, *being born in the likeness of men,* namely, according to species: "Therefore he had to be made like his brethren in every respect" (Heb. 2:17). If you say that it is not fitting to speak of a species in the Lord Jesus Christ: it is true in the sense that a new species does not arise from His divinity and humanity, as though His divinity and humanity agreed in having one common species of nature, for it would follow that His divine nature, so to say, would have changed.

Thirdly, he mentions the conditions of His human nature when he says, *and being found in human form.* For He assumed all the defects and properties associated with the human species, except sin; therefore, he says, *and being found in human form,* namely, in His external life, because He became hungry as a man and tired and so on: "One who in every respect has been tempted as we are, yet without sinning" (Heb. 4:15); "Afterward [He] appeared upon earth and lived among men" (Bar. 3:37). Thus, we can refer *form* to outward activities. Or *in human form* [*in habit*], because He put humanity on as a habit. For there are four kinds of habit [*habitus*] or ways in which something is "had": one "had thing" changes a person without itself being changed, as a fool by wisdom; another is changed and also changes the possessor, as food; a third neither changes the possessor nor is changed, as a ring worn on the finger; another is changed and does not change the possessor, as a dress. And by this likeness the human nature in Christ is called a habit or "something had"; because it comes to the divine person without changing it, but the nature itself was changed for the better, because it was filled with grace and truth: "We have beheld his glory, glory as of the only Son from the Father" (Jn. 1:14). He says, therefore, *being born in the likeness of men,* but in such a way that He is not changed, because in habit He was found as a man.

It should be noted that some have fallen into error on account of this phrase, *being found in human form.* Hence he touches on several opinions: the first is that Christ's humanity accrues to Him as an accident. This is false, because the person existing in the divine nature became a person existing in the human nature; therefore, it is present not as an accident, but substantially: not that the humanity is united to the Word in His nature, but in His person. By this is excluded the error of Photinus, who said that Christ was true man but not of the Virgin: however, Paul says, *he was in the form of God;* therefore, He was in the form of God before receiving the form of a servant, as a result of which He is less than the Father, because He *did not count equality with God a thing to be grasped.* Arius' error is also excluded, for he said Christ was less than the Father; but Paul says, He *did not count equality with God a thing to be grasped.* And Nestorius' error, who said that the union should be taken as an indwelling, so that God dwells in the Son of man as in a temple, and that the Son of man is a person distinct from the Son of God. And Rabanus says that the incarnation was an emptying. Now it is evident that the Father and the Holy Spirit are involved in every indwelling; therefore, they too are emptied. But this is false. Furthermore, Paul says, *He emptied himself;* therefore the person emptied and the one emptying are the same. But this is the Son, because He emptied Himself. Therefore, the union is in the person. Also the error of Eutyches, who said that one nature results from the two. Therefore, He did not receive the form of a servant, but a different one, which is contrary to what the Apostle says. Also the error of Valentinus, who said that He took His body from heaven; and the error of Appollinaris, who said that He had no soul. If this were so, He would not have been *born in the likeness of man.*

Then when he says, He *humbled himself,* he commends Christ's humility as indicated in His passion: first, he shows Christ's humility; secondly, its manner (2:8). Therefore He was man, but very great, because the same one is God and man; yet He *humbled himself:* "The greater you are, the more you must humble yourself" (Si. 3:18); "Learn from me, for I am gentle and lowly in heart" (Matt. 11:29).

The manner and the sign of His humility is obedience, whereas it is characteristic of the proud to follow their own will, for a proud person seeks greatness. But it pertains to a great thing that it not be ruled by something else, but that it rule other things; therefore, obedience is contrary to pride.

Hence, in order to show the greatness of Christ's humility and passion, he says that He *became obedient;* because if He had not suffered out of obedience, His passion would not be so commendable, for obedience gives merit to our sufferings. But how was He made obedient? Not by His divine will, because it is a rule; but by His human will, which is ruled in all things according to the Father's will: "Nevertheless, not as I will but as thou wilt" (Mt. 26:39). And it is fitting that He bring obedience into His passion, because the first sin was accomplished by disobedience: "For as by one man's disobedience many were made sinners, so by one man's obedience many will be made righteous" (Rom. 5:19); ["The obedient man shall speak of victory" (Prov. 21:28)]. That this obedience is great and commendable is evident from the fact that obedience is great when it follows the will of another against one's own. Now the movement of the human will tends toward two things, namely, to life and to honor. But Christ did not refuse death: "Christ also died for sins once for all, the righteous for the unrighteous" (1 Pet. 3:18). Furthermore, He did not flee ignominy; hence he says, *even death on a cross,* which is the most shameful: "Let us condemn him to a shameful death" (Wis. 2:20). Thus, He neither refused death nor an ignominous form of death.

2–3

9 Therefore God has highly exalted him and bestowed on him the name which is above every name, 10 that at the name of Jesus every knee should bow, in heaven and on earth and under the earth, 11 and every tongue confess that Jesus Christ is Lord, to the glory of God the Father. 12 Therefore, my beloved, as you have always obeyed, so now, now only as in my presence but much more in my absence, work out your own salvation with fear and trembling; 13 for God is at work in you, both to will and to work for his good pleasure.

Above he praised Christ's humility, here he cites its reward, which is exaltation and glory: "Every one who exalts himself will be humbled, and he who humbles himself will be exalted" (Lk. 14.11); "God save the lowly" (Job 22:29). Note the three-fold exaltation of Christ. First, as to the glory of the resurrection (2:9a); secondly, as to the manifestation of His divinity (2:9b); thirdly, as to the reverence shown by every creature (2:10).

He says, *therefore God has highly exalted him,* namely, that He should rise from the dead and pass from mortality to immortality: "Christ being raised from the dead will never die again; death no longer has dominion over him" (Rom. 6:9); "The right hand of the Lord does valiantly! I shall not die, but I shall live" (Ps. 118:16). He also exalted Him by setting Him on His right hand: "He raised him from the dead and made him sit at his right hand in the heavenly places, far above all rule and authority and power and dominion, and above every name that is named, not only in this age but also in that which is to come" (Eph. 1:20). But while it is true that others are raised to glory and immortality, He is more so, because God *bestowed on him the name which is above every name.* Now a name is imposed to signify some thing, and the loftier the thing signified by a name, the loftier is the name: hence the name of the divinity is highest: "O Lord, our Lord, how majestic is thy name in all the earth!" (Ps. 8:1). Therefore, this name, that He should be called and should be God, the Father gave Him, i.e., to Christ, as to the true God.

But Photinus says that this is mentioned here as a reward for Christ's humility and that it does not mean He is true God, but merely that He received a certain pre-eminence over the creature and a likeness of the godhead. This however, is not true, because it was stated that *he was in the form of God.* Therefore, one must answer that there are two natures and one hypostasis in Christ: for this person is God and man. Therefore, this can be explained in two ways: in one way, that the Father gave Him this name inasmuch as He is the Son of God; and this from all eternity by an eternal engendering, so that this giving is no more than His eternal generation: "For as the Father has life in himself, so he has granted the Son also to have life in himself" (Jn. 5:26). In another way it can refer to

Christ as man; and then the Father gave that man the name
of being God not by nature, because God's nature is distinct
from the nature of man, but to be God by the grace, not of
adoption, but of union, by which He is at once God and man:
"Designated Son of God in power," He, namely, "who was descended from David according to the flesh" (Rom. 1:4). This
second way is Augustine's explanation in keeping with the
Apostle's intention. Similarly, it is stated in Acts (2:36) "Let
all the house of Israel therefore know assuredly that God has
made him both Lord and Christ, this Jesus whom you crucified."
The first is Ambrose's.

But you might object to both explanations and ask why he
says, *he humbled himself and became obedient unto death*
and follows with, *therefore God has hightly exalted him*, since
the reward does not precede the merit. Therefore, neither the
eternal engendering nor the incarnation is the reward of Christ's
passion, because they precede it. The answer is that in Sacred
Scripture a thing is said to occur when it is known. Therefore,
God bestowed, i.e., made manifest to the world, that He has
this name. This was manifested in the resurrection, because
prior to it the divinity of Christ was not that well known. This
is supported by the text which follows: it implies that He did
not give Him a name He did not already have, but that all
should venerate it. And he mentions two types of veneration,
namely, subjecting the body and confessing with the mouth:
and every tongue confess. He says therefore: He has given Him
a name which is above all names, even as man; hence he adds,
that at the name of Jesus, which is the name of the man, *every
knee should bow*; "To me every knee shall bow, every tongue
shall swear" (Is. 45:23).

But here is where Origen erred, because when he heard that
every knee should bow, which is a sign of subjection, he believed that at some future time every rational creature, whether
angels or men or devils, would be subjected to Christ by the
allegiance of charity. But this is contrary to Matthew (25:41):
"Depart from me, you cursed, into the eternal fire prepared for
the devil and his angels." It should be noted that there are two
kinds of subjection: one is voluntary and the other involuntary.

In the future it will come about that all the holy angels will be subject to Christ voluntarily; hence he says, *every knee should bow,* where he mentions the sign for the thing signified: ["Adore him all his angels" (Ps. 96:8)]. Likewise, holy and just and beatified men will be subject in this way: "All the nations thou has made shall come and bow down before thee, O Lord, and shall glorify thy name" (Ps. 86:9); but not the devils and the damned, for they will be subject involuntarily: "Even the demons believe—and shudder" (Jas. 2:19).

Then when he says, *and every tongue confess,* he touches on the reverence shown by confessing with the mouth: *Every tongue,* namely, *in heaven and on earth and under the earth.* This does not refer to a confession of praise from those under the earth, but to a forced confession, which is made by recognizing God: "And the glory of the Lord shall be revealed, and all flesh shall see it together" (Is. 40:5); "Let them praise thy great and terrible name! holy is he!" (Ps. 99:3). And this confession will recognize *that Jesus Christ is Lord [in] the glory of God the Father.* He does not say in a similar glory, because it is the same glory: "That all may honor the Son, even as they honor the Father?" (Jn. 5:23). It should be noted that earlier he had said that, *he was in the form of God,* but here he says *in the glory,* because it would come to pass that what He had from all eternity would be known by all: "Father, glorify thou me in thy own presence with the glory which I had with thee before the world was made" (Jn. 17:5).

Then when he says, *Therefore, my beloved,* the exhortation is brought to an end. In regard to this he does three things: first, he exhorts them to act well; secondly, how to do so (2:14); thirdly, with what fruit (2:15). The first part is divided into three: first, he recalls their past obedience; secondly, he shows what they should do (2:12); thirdly, he gives them confidence in accomplishing this (2:13).

He says, therefore: Since Christ thus humbled Himself and was exalted for it, you ought to realize that if you are humbled, you shall also be exalted; and you should do this *as you have always obeyed.* He recalls their obedience to show its relevance to good works, because every virtue is included under obedience. For a man is just inasmuch as he keeps God's commandments: "Do you not know that if you yield yourself to anyone as obedient slaves, you are slaves of the one whom you obey, either of sin, which leads to death, or of obedience, which leads to righteousness?" (Rom. 6:16). Furthermore, every good work, no matter how good it is of itself, is made better by obedience; ["The obedient man shall speak of victories" (Prov. 21:28)]. Finally, obedience is one of the greatest of the virtues: for to offer something from one's external things is great; to offer something from the body is greater; but the greatest is to offer something from your soul and will: and this is done by obedience: "To obey is better than sacrifice, and to hearken than the fat of rams" (1 Sam. 15:22). If you have acted thus, I urge you to continue doing the same.

Then when he says, *not only as in my presence,* he shows what they should do. First, he urges them to act faithfully, because an unfaithful servant serves only when the master is looking, because he seeks only to please; but a faithful servant always works well. Hence he says, *not only as in my presence,* for then it would appear that you are not acting from the instinct of good will: "Not in the way of eye-service, as men-pleasers, but as servants of Christ, doing the will of God from the heart" (Eph. 6:6). Secondly, that they act humbly, when he says, *with fear and trembling,* for the proud man does not fear, but the humble does: "Let anyone who thinks that he stands take heed lest he fall" (1 Cor. 10:12); "Blessed is the man who fears the Lord always" (Prov. 28:14); "Serve the Lord with fear, with trembling kiss his feet" (Ps. 2:11). Thirdly, that they act with an eye toward salvation: *work out your own salvation:* "He who endures to the end will be saved" (Mt. 24:13).

Then when he says, *for God is at work in you, both to will and to work,* he strengthens their confidence, and he excludes four false opinions: the first is the opinion of those who believe that man can be saved by his own free will without God's help. Against this he says: *For God is at work in you, both to will and to work:* "The Father who dwells in me does his works" (Jn. 14:10); "Apart from me you can do nothing" (Jn. 15:5).

The second are those who deny free will altogether and say that man is necessitated by fate or by divine providence. He excludes this when he says, *in you,* because He moves the will from within to act well: "Thou has wrought for us all our works" (Is. 26:12). The third, like the first, is that of the Pelagians who say that choices are in us, but the performing of works in God, because willing comes from us, but accomplishing comes from God. He excludes this when he says, *both to will and to work:* "It depends not upon man's will," i.e., without God's help, "or exertion, but upon God's mercy" (Rom. 9:16). The fourth is the opinion that God accomplishes every good in us and does this through our merits. He excludes this when he says [*according to*] *for his good pleasure,* and not our merits, because before we get God's grace there is no good merit in us: "Do good to Zion in thy good pleasure" (Ps. 51:18).

2–4

14 Do all things without grumbling or questioning, 15 that you may be blameless and innocent, children of God without blemish in the midst of a crooked and perverse generation, among whom you shine as lights in the world, 16 holding fast the word of life, so that in the day of Christ I may be proud that I did not run in vain or labor in vain. 17 Even if I am to be poured as a libation upon the sacrificial offering of your faith, I am glad and rejoice with you all. 18 Likewise you also should be glad and rejoice with me. 19 I hope in the Lord Jesus to send Timothy to you soon, so that I may be cheered by news of you. 20 I have no one like him, who will be genuinely anxious for your welfare. 21 They all look after their own interests, not those of Jesus Christ. 22 But Timothy's worth you know, how as a son with a father he has served with me in the gospel. 23 I hope therefore to send him just as soon as I see how it will go with me; 24 and I trust in the Lord that shortly I myself shall come also. 25 I have thought it necessary to send to you Epaphroditus my brother and fellow worker and fellow

soldier, and your messenger and minister to my need, 26 for
he has been longing for you all, and has been distressed because
you heard that he was ill. 27 Indeed he was ill, near to death.
But God had mercy on him, and not only on him but on me
also, lest I should have sorrow upon sorrow. 28 I am the more
eager to send him, therefore, that you may rejoice at seeing him
again, and that I may be less anxious. 29 So receive him in the
Lord with all joy; and honor such men, 30 for he nearly died
for the work of Christ, risking his life to complete your service
to me.

Above, the Apostle exhorted them to do works leading to
salvation; here he teaches them how. First, he teaches them the
way to do these works; secondly, he gives the reason (2:15).

First, he points out two ways to act, namely, *without grumbling or questioning*. For virtuous works are very difficult, and
offer a fertile field for grumbling: "We must not grumble, as
some of them did and were destroyed by the Destroyer" (1 Cor.
10:10). Furthermore, they should not hesitate about doing
them: "He who doubts is like a wave of the sea that is driven
and tossed by the wind" (Jas. 1:6).

He gives reasons for this: first, on their part, and then on
the part of the Apostle. On their part he gives three reasons:
first, in regard to the faithful when he says, *that you may be
blameless:* "Walking in all the commandments and ordinances
of the Lord blameless" (Lk. 1:6). For no one can exist without
sin, but he can without grumbling; hence he urges them to do
this. Secondly, in regard to God, *and innocent children of God.*
For a son is like his Father. But God is innocent; hence we
are innocent sons of God, when our intention is directed to one
object: "A double-minded man is unstable in all his ways" (Jas.
1:8); "Be as wise as serpents and innocent as doves" (Mt.
10:16). Thirdly, in regard to unbelievers, *without blemish*, i.e.,
behave well toward unbelievers and give no offense *in the midst
of a crooked*, as to evil works, *and perverse generation*, as to
unbelief. And this is when they cannot be defamed by them:
"Give the enemy no occasion to revile us" (1 Tim. 5:14). He
gives the reason for this when he says, *among whom you shine*

as lights in the world, because no matter how the world changes, the lights of the world remain bright: "You are the light of the world" (Mt. 5:14). They are luminous, not in essence, because God alone is light in this way: "The life was the light of man" (Jn. 1:4). The same is true of the saints: "He was not the light" (Jn. 1:8).

But they are light inasmuch as they have some of that light which was the light of men, i.e., of the Word of God radiating on us. Therefore he says, *holding fast the word of life,* i.e., the word of Christ: "Lord, to whom shall we go? You have the words of eternal life" (Jn. 6:69); "Thy word is a lamp to my feet and a light to my path" (Ps. 119:105).

Then he gives a reason on the part of the Apostle: *so that I may be proud;* secondly, he explains the reason, because subjects should act well so as to redound to the glory of their prelates. For it is their glory, when subjects are well behaved: "A wise son makes a glad father" (Prov. 10:1); "You are our glory and joy" (1 Thess. 2:20). And this, *in the day of Christ,* namely, when He will lead His faithful to Himself. This redounds to his glory for two reasons; because of the labor and suffering he endured in preaching. Therefore, he says, *that I did not run in vain or labor in vain.* He calls preaching a running because of his agility in traveling from Jerusalem to Spain. He says *labor,* because of the contradictions and punishments he suffered; and this not in vain, but in much fruit: "His grace toward me was not in vain" (1 Cor. 15:10).

He refers to his suffering when he says, *even if I am to be poured as a libation upon the sacrificial offering of your faith.* For in converting others he offers to God a sacrifice of those he converts. But sometimes tyrants mingle the blood of the offerers with their sacrifices, as in Luke (13:0); hence he says, I offer God the sacrifice of your faith. And if it turn out that I myself am immolated, i.e., killed, by reason of offering the sacrifice of your conversion, *I am glad* on my part: "Count it all joy, my brethren, when you meet various trials" (Jas. 1:2), *and rejoice with you all,* that you have the faith, even with danger to my person with whom you rejoice in this too; hence he says, *likewise you also should be glad and rejoice with me:* "Rejoice with those who rejoice" (Rom. 12:15).

Then when he says, *I hope in the Lord Jesus to send Timothy to you soon,* he proposes his own disciples as an example: first, Timothy and then, Epaphroditus. In regard to the first he does three things: first, he promises to send Timothy; secondly, he commends him (2:20); thirdly, he hints at the time he will send him (2:23).

He says, therefore, *I hope in the Lord Jesus to send Timothy to you soon.* Here it should be noted that the Apostle has such trust in God that he attributes the slightest things to God: "Not that we are sufficient of ourselves to claim anything as coming from us; our sufficiency is from God" (2 Cor. 3:5). The text is clear.

Then he praises him: first, on account of his love for them, and secondly, because of his devotion to the Apostle. Thus he makes a good mediator, because he loves them and he venerates him. He says: I am sending Timothy because *I have no one like him,* i.e., so interested in your progress: ["He makes men of one way to dwell in one house" (Ps. 67:7)] *who will be genuinely anxious for your welfare. Genuinely anxious,* because it is for God alone: "We are as men of sincerity, as commissioned by God, in the sight of God we speak in Christ" (2 Cor. 2:17). The reason why I have no one of the same mind is because *all look after their own interests, not those of Jesus Christ,* i.e., they do not seek things pertaining to the salvation of their neighbor and the glory of God, but pertaining to their profit and glory and themselves.

But did Luke and Epaphroditus and the others, who were with the Apostle seek the things that were their own? I answer that in the company of the Apostle were many who sought this and who deserted him: "For Demas, in love with this present world, has deserted me and gone to Thessalonica; Crescens has gone to Galatia, Titus to Dalmatia. Luke alone is with me" (2 Tim. 4:9). But it is a custom that sometimes the Scripture speaks of some as though of all: "From the least to the greatest of them, every one is greedy for unjust gains and from prophet

to priest, every one deals falsely" (Jer. 6:13). Therefore it is
a narrowed use of the word "all."

And if you would know how he has behaved in regard to me,
I answer that, *Timothy's worth you know, how as a son with
a father he has served with me in the gospel,* i.e., as though he
were a special son: "I sent to you Timothy, my beloved and
faithful child in the Lord" (1 Cor. 4:17). *I hope therefore to
send him,* so solicitous for you and so dear to me.

But why not at once? Because it is otherwise with Christ and
with the other saints. In Christ was fulness of grace; hence He
always had knowledge of all things; but not so the other saints.
Hence the Apostle foresaw some things about himself and was
ignorant of others. Thus, he received no revelation that he
would be delivered from his imprisonment; hence he says, *just
as soon as I see how it will go with me,* because if I were
granted leave, I would come to you in person; consequently,
I trust in the Lord that shortly I myself shall come also. But
he was not freed from his prison: "Yea, thou dost light my
lamp: the Lord my God lightens my darkness" (Ps. 18:28). For
there is always some darkness in the saints.

Then when he says, *I have thought it necessary,* he proposes
another disciple as an example, namely, Epaphroditus. First,
he describes him; secondly, he suggests how he should be
received (2:29). In regard to the first he does three things:
first, he praises him; secondly, he states the reason why he is
sending him (2:26); thirdly, he explains it (2:27).

He says, therefore: *I have thought it necessary to send to you
Epaphroditus, my brother and fellow worker and fellow soldier,
and your messenger and minister to my need.* He calls him his
brother on account of the Father: "You are all brethren" (Mt.
23:8); *and fellow worker,* i.e., in the work of preaching: "A
brother helped is like a strong city" (Prov. 18:19); *and fellow
soldier,* because we have suffered tribulation together: "Take
your share of suffering as a good soldier of Christ Jesus" (2 Tim.
2:3); and *your messenger,* i.e., teacher. He was the bishop of
the Philippians and sent by them to serve the Apostle; hence
he says, *and minister to my need:* "I am filled, having received

from Epaphroditus the things you sent, a fragrant offering, a sacrifice, acceptable and pleasing to God" (*infra* 4:18). But why? To satisfy the desire with which *he has been longing for you all:* "For I long to see you" (Rom. 1:11), and also to relieve him of his sorrow, because he was sad at the sorrow you felt, when you heard that he was sick. He explains the reason, saying: *Indeed he was ill, near to death,* i.e., in the opinion of the physicians, though not according to God's providence, but for the glory of God; "This illness is not unto death; it is for the glory of God" (Jn. 11:4). Thus he continues: *but God had mercy on him;* "Be gracious to me, O Lord, for I am languishing" (Ps. 6:2); *and not only on him but on me also,* because Paul had suffered the temporal and natural sadness of his affliction, as Christ is said to have suffered sometimes.

Then he concludes by indicating how he should be received and why. He should be received honorably in the Lord, whose minister he is: "You received me as an angel of God, as Christ Jesus" (Gal. 4:14); "Let the elders who rule well be considered worthy of double honor, especially those who labor in preaching and teaching" (1 Tim. 5:17). And this because *he nearly died for the work of Christ,* i.e., for God and the salvation of the faithful: "Greater love has no man than this, that a man lay down his life for his friends" (Jn. 15:13); *risking his life:* "The good shepherd lays down his life for the sheep" (Jn. 10:11). And he did this, *to complete your service to me,* which you personally could not do.

3–1

1 Finally, my brethren, rejoice in the Lord. To write the same things to you is not irksome to me, and is safe for you. 2 Look out for the dogs, look out for the evil-workers, look out for those who mutilate the flesh. 3 For we are the true circumcision, who worship God in spirit, and glory in Christ Jesus, and put no confidence in the flesh. 4 Though I myself have reason for confidence in the flesh also. If any other man thinks he has reason for confidence in the flesh, I have more: 5 circumcised on the

eighth day, of the people of Israel, of the tribe of Benjamin, a Hebrew born of Hebrews; as to the law a Pharisee, 6 as to zeal a persecutor of the church, as to righteousness under the law blameless. 7 But whatever gain I had, I counted as loss for the sake of Christ. 8 Indeed I count everything as loss because of the surpassing worth of knowing Christ Jesus my Lord. For his sake I have suffered the loss of all things, and count them as refuse, in order that I may gain Christ 9 and be found in him.

Above, he proposed the example they should follow; here he shows whose example they should avoid. In regard to this he does three things: first, he mentions whom they should avoid; secondly, the examples the saints gave of avoiding (3:3); thirdly, he urges them to avoid those whom they considered worthy of imitation. The first is divided into three parts: first, he mentions the purpose of his doctrine; secondly, why he must write (3:1); thirdly, the reason it is necessary (3:2).

The aim of the admonition is to keep the Gentile believers from the ceremonies of the Law, to which certain persons were persuading them; hence he says *finally*, i.e., after my warnings, *my brethren*, namely, in the faith, *rejoice in the Lord* only, and not in the ceremonies of the Law: "I will rejoice in the Lord, I will joy in the God of my salvation" (Hab. 3:18). And this because it *is not irksome to me to write* in my absence *the same things* I said when I was present. For words soon pass away, but writings endure: "The wisdom of the scribe depends on the opportunity of leisure; and he who has little business may become wise" (Si. 38:24); "Beloved, being very eager to write to you of our common salvation, I found it necessary to write" (Jude 1:3); "But on some points I have written to you very boldly by way of reminder" (Rom. 15:15).

The need for this admonition is that certain seducers are busy; therefore, he must be busier in writing to them; hence he says, *look out for the dogs, look out for the evil-workers.* He mentions three things about them: first, the unreasoning cruelty of their hearts; hence he says *dogs:* "It is the nature of a dog to bark from anger, not from reason but from habit" (Gloss). These people do the same: "The dogs have a mighty appetite;

they never have enough. The shepherds also have no understanding; they have all turned to their own way" (Is. 56:11); "Outside are the dogs and sorcerers" (Rev. 22:15). Secondly, the perverse doctrine they sow: *evil-workers,* because they do not labor faithfully in the Lord's vineyard or sow good seed in the soil: "An enemy has done this" (Mt. 13:28); "Do your best to present yourself to God as one approved, a workman who has no need to be ashamed, rightly handling the word of truth" (2 Tim. 2:15). Thirdly, he mentions their error: *those who mutilate the flesh* [*concession*]. He uses this word to describe their mark, for they preach circumcision, which seeks to rival Christ's grace: "If you receive circumcision, Christ will be of no advantage to you" (Gal. 5:2). Hence playing on the word, he says *concision,* as though they had not circumcision, but a cut.

Then when he says, *for we are the true circumcision,* he shows how they should be avoided by the saints: first, how they are avoided by others; secondly, by himself: (3:4).

He says, therefore: I say that they are *those who mutilate the flesh,* but *we who worship God are the true circumcision.* For circumcision is of two kinds, namely, bodily and spiritual: "For he is not a real Jew who is one outwardly, nor is true circumcision something external and physical. He is a Jew who is one inwardly, and real circumcision is a matter of the heart, spiritual and not literal" (Rom. 2:28). For the circumcision of the flesh cuts off superfluous flesh; but the circumcision of the spirit is that by which the Holy Spirit cuts away superfluous internal concupiscences. Therefore, he says: *We are the true circumcision, who worship God in spirit,* i.e., who circumcises us inwardly to God. "For God is my witness, whom I serve with my spirit in the gospel of his Son" (Rom. 1:9); "I will sing with the spirit and I will sing with the mind also" (1 Cor. 14:15). But circumcision is given as a sign of Abraham's faith, to show that his faith, which believed in an offspring to come, was true: "The promises were made to Abraham and to his offspring" (Gal. 3:16). Therefore, circumcision is a sign of Abraham's faith in Christ. Consequently, he is circumcised who by the Holy Spirit is renewed inwardly in Christ, who is the truth of the circumcision: "In him also you were circumcised with a circumcision made without hands" (Col. 2:11). *We put no confidence in the flesh*, i.e., in the circumcision of the flesh, because, as it is stated in John (6:63): "It is the spirit that gives life, the flesh is no avail." The word "flesh" is sometimes taken for fleshly concupiscence, sometimes for the care of the flesh, and sometimes for observances of the flesh.

Then when he says, *though I myself have reason for confidence in the flesh also,* he gives his own example: first, he mentions the prestige he had under the Law; secondly, he shows how he scorned it (3:7). In regard to the first he does two things: first, he makes a general statement; secondly, he explains it part by part (3:5).

In regard to the first he does two things: first, he shows the confidence he could have had in the things of the Law, saying: We must not put our confidence in the things of the Law, *though I myself have reason for confidence in the flesh also,* i.e., I could have, if I desired, because "Whatever anyone dares to boast of—I am speaking as a fool—I also dare to boast of that," as he says in 2 Corinthians (11:21). And I can do this with more reason, because I have done more: "I am talking like a madman" (2 Cor. 11:23). He mentions all these things in order more effectively to destroy the observances of the Law. For many scorn things they do not know or do not have; and this is not right, but only when a person has something and then scorns it and does not glory in it. Thus, if the Apostle had no prestige during the time of the Law, this could be cited as the reason why he went over to the gospel. Therefore, he shows the prestige he had under the Law: first, in general, and secondly, according to the life he led: *as to the Law a Pharisee.* As to the first, in three ways: first, in regard to the sacrament of his race, because he was *circumcised on the eighth day:* "It shall be a sign of the covenant between me and you" (Gen. 17:11). He says *on the eighth day* because this was the difference between proselytes and the descendants of Abraham: the former were not circumcised on the eighth day, but as adults, when they were converted; but the latter on the eighth day according to the Law: "He that is eight days old among you shall be circumcised" (Gen. 17:12). Thus it was not as a proselyte but as a true Israelite that he was circumcised. Secondly, in regard to his race when he says, *of the people of Israel.* For two races descended from Abraham: one through Isaac, and the other through Ismael. From Isaac also two races descended: one through Esau and one through Jacob. But the one from Esau and the one from Ismael were not included in the inheritance, but only Jacob who is also called Israel; hence he says, *of the people of Israel:* "Are they Israelites? So am I" (2 Cor. 11:22).

Then in regard to his tribe, because in the tribe of Israel some were descended from bondwomen, i.e., from Bala and Zelpha, and some from free women, namely, Lia and Rachel. Among these some persevered in the worship of God, namely, the tribes of Levi, Juda and Benjamin, but the others turned to idols during the time of Jeroboam. Therefore, the *tribe of Benjamin* was privileged, because it continued in the faith and worship of God, and the temple was built in it: "The beloved of the Lord, he dwells in safety by him; he encompasses him all the day long, and makes his dwelling between his shoulders" (Deut. 33:12); "Benjamin is a ravenous wolf, in the morning devouring the prey, and at evening dividing the spoil" (Gen. 49:27). He prefigured Paul who in his early days persecuted the Church. Thirdly, in regard to his name and tongue when he says, *a Hebrew.* Some say that the word "Hebrew" comes from Abraham, as Augustine did, but later retracted. But it is taken from Heber (Gen. 11:16). That it does not come from Abraham is evident, because Abraham himself is called a Hebrew: "Then one who had escaped came, and told Abram the Hebrew" (Gen. 14:13). A gloss on Genesis (11) says that in the time of Heber the languages of all nations were separated, but the primitive language remained in the family of Heber and in the worship of the one God and among all the Hebrews. He was also born of Hebrew parents; hence he says, *born of Hebrews.*

Then he shows the prestige he had in his manner of life: first of all, in regard to his sect when he says, *as to the law a Pharisee.* For there were three sects among the Jews, namely, the Pharisees, the Sadducees, and the Essenes. But the Pharisees were closer to the truth, because the Sadducees denied the resurrection and did not believe in angels or spirits, while the Pharisees believed both, as it is stated in Acts (23). For this reason the sect of the Pharisees was more commendable. That he was a Pharisee is stated in Acts (26:5): "According to the strictest party of our religion I have lived as a Pharisee." Secondly, in regard to the zeal which the Jews had, although not according to knowledge, in persecuting Christians; hence he says, *a persecutor of the church.* "He who once persecuted us is now preaching the faith he once tried to destroy" (Gal. 1:23); "I myself was convinced that I ought to do many things in opposing the name of Jesus of Nazareth. And I did so in Jerusalem" (Acts 26:9); "I am unfit, to be called an Apostle because I persecuted the church of God" (1 Cor. 15:9).

Thirdly, in regard to the innocence of his manner of life; hence he says, *as to righteousness under the Law blameless.* This justice consists in externals, but the justice of faith is of the heart: "God who knows the heart . . . cleanse their hearts by faith" (Acts 15:9). As to external justice the Apostle lived innocently; hence he says, *blameless.* He does not say "without sin," because blame is concerned with a sin of scandal against one's neighbor in matters that are external: "And they were both righteous before God, walking in all the commandments and ordinances of the Lord blameless" (Lk. 1:6). Therefore, he does not contradict what he says in Ephesians (2:3): "Among these we all once lived," because he did not then have the true justice of faith, which makes a man pure, but only the justice of the Law.

Then when he says, *but whatever gain I had,* he shows his contempt for the prestige he had under the Law: first, he shows in general why he scorned the things of the Law; secondly, in detail (3:8).

He says, therefore: *Whatever gain I had,* i.e., prestige, namely, to be a Pharisee and so on, *I counted as loss for the sake of Christ,* i.e., I came to regard them as hindrances. For the observances of the Law, which were effective during the time of the Law, became harmful after Christ; hence he says, *loss.* And the reason for abandoning them was Christ; hence he says, *for the sake of Christ*. He explains this: first, that he acted thus in order to know Christ, and secondly to obtain Him. In regard to the first he says, *Indeed I count everything as loss*. This is true, if he had continued to depend on them. What I did formerly, I now regard a loss on account of my desire for a correct understanding of Christ, my Lord: "For I decided to know nothing among you except Jesus Christ and him crucified" (1 Cor. 2:2). *Because of the surpassing worth of knowing Christ Jesus my Lord*, since this transcends all knowledge. For there is nothing better to be known than the Word of God "in whom are hid all the treasures of wisdom and knowledge" (Col. 2:3).

In regard to the second he says, *for his sake I have suffered the loss of all things*. First, he shows that he scorned the observance of the Law in order to obtain Christ; secondly, how he could obtain Christ: *not having a righteousness of my own, based on Law*. He says, therefore: *I have suffered the loss of all things* by regarding them as vile and contemptible, *that I may gain Christ*, i.e., obtain Him and be united to Him by charity.

3–2

9b Not having a righteousness of my own, based on law, but that which is through faith in Christ, the righteousness from God that depends on faith; 10 that I may know him and the power of his resurrection, and may share his sufferings, becoming like him in his death, 11 that if possible I may attain the resurrection from the dead. 12 Not that I have already obtained this or am already perfect; but I press on to make it my own, because Christ Jesus has made me his own. 13 Brethren, I do not consider that I have made it my own; but one thing I do, forgetting what lies behind and straining forward to what lies ahead, 14 I press on toward the goal for the prize of the upward call of God in Christ Jesus.

Above, he showed that he scorned past gains for the sake of Christ, that is, in order to know and win Christ; here he intends to explain these things: first, how he desires to gain Christ and be found in Him by justice; secondly, by enduring sufferings (3:10). In regard to the first, he does two things: first, he shows which justice he abandoned; secondly, which one he now seeks (3:9).

It should be noted that justice is taken sometimes as the special virtue through which a man fulfills what is right in matters pertaining to life in society, in the sense that it directs a person in this matter; for temperance deals with one's own internal passions, but justice deals with another person. In another way justice is a general virtue, inasmuch as a man observes the law for the common good. This is the sense in which it is used in Scripture for the observance of the divine law: "I have done what is just and right" i.e., the law (Ps. 119:121), which he obeyed out of love, as though moved by his own initiative. In this way it is a virtue, but not if he is moved in some other way, such as by an external cause or for the sake of gain or because of punishments, where to obey might be personally displeasing. According to this there are two kinds of justice: one is moral justice; the other is legal justice, which makes one obey the law not from love but from fear. Therefore he says, *not having a righteousness of my own, based on law,* because as Augustine says: "The slight difference between the Law and the Gospel is fear and love"; "For you did not receive the spirit of slavery to fall back into fear, but you have received the spirit of sonship" (Rom. 8:15).

But if your righteousness is your own, how is it from the Law? I answer that it is indeed mine, because I accomplish such works with human power without the inward vesture of sanctifying grace; but it is from the Law as from the one teaching. Or, it is mine to presume to obey it by myself: "Moses writes that the man who practices the righteousness which is based on the law shall live by it" (Rom. 15:5).

Concerning this justice which he seeks, he states three things, namely, the method of acquiring it; its author; and its fruit. The method is that it is not obtained except by faith in Christ: "Since we are justified by faith, we have peace with God through our Lord, Jesus Christ" (Rom. 5:1); "The righteousness of God through faith in Jesus Christ for all who believe" (Rom. 3:22). For the author is God and not man: "It is God who justifies" (Rom. 8:33); "And to one who does not work but trusts him who justifies the ungodly, his faith is reckoned as righteousness" (Rom. 4:5). Therefore he says, *the righteousness from God that depends on faith:* "The Holy Spirit whom God has given to those who obey him" (Acts 5:32). The fruit is knowledge of Him and the power of His resurrection and to be in the company of His saints.

These things can be explained in two ways according to the two forms of knowledge: in one way, in terms of knowledge available in this life. In that case one must know three things about Him: first, His person, namely, that He is true God and true man; hence he says, *that I may know him:* "Have I been with you so long, and yet you do not know me, Philip? He who has seen me has seen the Father" (Jn. 14:9). Secondly, the glory of His resurrection; hence he says, *and the power of his resurrection,* i.e., the powerful resurrection performed by His own power. Thirdly, how to imitate Him, when he says, *and may share his sufferings,* namely, be associated with Him in His passion: "Christ also suffered for you, leaving you an example, that you should follow in his steps" (1 Pet. 2:21). In the other way, by practical knowledge, which begins from what is later, which is the last thing accomplished but the first thing intended. The first thing intended is the knowledge of God through His essence, to which faith leads: "They shall all know me, from the least of them to the greatest" (Jer. 31:34); therefore, he says, *that I may know him.* Secondly that not only the soul will be glorified, but the body also; hence he says, *and the power of his resurrection,* namely, by which we shall rise: "If Christ has not been raised, then our preaching is in vain" (1 Cor. 15:14). Thirdly, the value of sharing His suffering, because we shall know how much it benefits us to be associated with His passion: "God is faithful, by whom you were called into the fellowship of his Son, Jesus Christ our Lord" (1 Cor. 1:9).

Then when he says, *becoming like him in his death,* he shows how he would like to grow and be found in Him by enduring

His sufferings: first, he mentions the endurance; secondly, its fruit (3:11).

He says, therefore: let me be found not only having justice but also conformed to his death, that I might suffer for justice and truth as Christ did: "I bear on my body the marks of Jesus" (Gal. 6:17). But its fruit is *that if possible I may attain the resurrection from the dead.* For one reaches glory by sufferings endured here: "For if we have been united with him in a death like his, we shall certainly be united with him in a resurrection like his" (Rom. 6:5); "If we have died with him, we shall also live with him" (2 Tim. 2:11); "Fellow heirs of God with Christ, provided we suffer with him" (Rom. 8:17). He says, *if possible,* because of its difficulty, arduousness and labor: "For the gate is narrow and the way is hard, that leads to life, and those who find it are few" (Mt. 7:14); "Prepare to meet your God, O Israel!" (Amos 4:12). For Christ rose by His own power, but man not by his own power, but by the grace of God: "He who raised Christ Jesus from the dead will give life to your mortal bodies also through his Spirit which dwells in you" (Rom. 8:11). Or it can refer to meeting the saints, when they shall meet Christ descending from heaven to judge.

Then when he says, *not that I have already obtained this,* he shows how his desire is deferred: first, he shows what he thinks of himself; secondly, he asks them to think the same thing of themselves (3:15). The first is divided into two parts: first, he shows how far short he is of the perfection intended; secondly, he explains this (3:13). In regard to the first he does two things: first, he shows that he has not arrived at perfection; secondly, that he is tending toward it (3:12b).

In tending toward it he seeks two things, namely, to obtain what he desires, and to enjoy it; for he would be seeking in vain, if he were not to enjoy it and inhere in it; therefore he says, *not that I have already obtained,* namely, the glory I seek: "But the righteous live forever . . . therefore they will receive a glorious crown and a beautiful diadem from the hand of the Lord" (Wis. 5:16); *or am already perfect:* "When the perfect comes, the imperfect will pass away" (1 Cor. 13:10).

But this attitude is contrary to the command to be perfect

(Mt. 5:48) and (Gen. 17:1). I answer that perfection is two-fold, namely, of heaven and of earth. For man's perfection consists in adhering to God through charity, because a thing is perfect to the degree it adheres to its perfection. But the soul can adhere to God in two ways: in one way, perfectly, so that a person actually refers his actions to God and knows Him as He can be known; and this is in heaven. But adherence in this life is of two kinds: one is necessary for salvation, and all are bound to it, namely, that a person in no case place his heart in anything against God, and that he habitually refer his whole life to Him. The Lord says of this way: "You shall love the Lord your God with all your heart, and with all your soul, and with all your mind" (Matt. 22:37). The other is of supererogation, when a person adheres to God above the common way. This is done when he removes his heart from temporal things, the better to approach heaven, because the smaller covetousness becomes, the more charity grows. Therefore, what is said here refers to the perfection of heaven.

Then when he says, *but I press on,* he shows his efforts toward it, saying, *I press on,* namely, after Christ: "He who follows me will not walk in darkness, but will have the light of life" (Jn. 8:12) and in (10:27): "My sheep hear my voice . . . and they follow me." And this, *to make it my own [to comprehend* Him]: "So run that you may obtain the prize" (1 Cor. 9:24).

But on the other hand God is incomprehensible, because it is said in Jeremiah (31:37): "If the heavens above can be measured, and the foundations of the earth below can be explored, then I will cast off all the descendants of Israel." I answer that in one sense, to comprehend means to enclose, as a house comprehends us; in another sense, it means to attain and hold. In the first sense He is incomprehensible, because He cannot be enclosed in a created intellect, since He is most simple and because you do not know or love Him to the degree that He is knowable and loveable, as a person who does not know a truth by demonstration but by opinion does not know it as perfectly as it can be known. But God knows Himself, as far as He is knowable. The reason for this is that a thing is known according to the mode of its own being and truth. God, however, is infinite light and truth, whereas our light is finite. Hence he says, *but I press on to make it my own*, that is, to comprehend Him in the second way, i.e., by attaining: "I held him, and would not let him go" (Cant. 3:4), *because Christ Jesus has made me his own.* This can be taken in three ways: for all glory depends on apprehending God, i.e., that God be present to our soul. But not all have equal happiness: because some see more clearly, just as some will love more ardently and will rejoice more. Hence each person will have a definite amount according to God's predestination; therefore, he says, *because Christ Jesus has made me his own.* As if to say: I intend to comprehend in such an amount as has been decided by Christ. Or, *I press on to make it my own*, as I am owned (apprehended). As if to say: that I may see Him as He sees me: "We shall see him as he is" (Jn. 3:2), not through a likeness, but through His essence. Or, *to make it my own*, by seeing Christ in glory, in which I am apprehended, i.e., in that glory in which He appeared, when I was converted.

Then when he says, *brethren, I do not consider. . . .* he explains what he had said: first, about his lack of perfection: secondly, the consequence (3:13b).

He says: *I do not consider that I have made it my own.* As if to say: I am not so vain as to attribute to myself something I do not yet have; but *I press on toward the goal.* This can be taken in three ways: In one way thus: *but one thing I do*, namely, *forgetting what lies behind . . . I press on toward the goal.* Or, *I do not consider that I have made it my own*, but *I press on toward* one thing, namely, *for the prize of the upward call of God in Christ Jesus.* Or, *I do not consider that I have made it my own*, namely, that which is above: "One thing have I asked of the Lord, that will I seek after" (Ps. 27:4). Then he shows what he deserted, namely, temporal things or past merits, because a man should not count his past merits.

Secondly, he shows what his destination is, namely, *straining forward to what lies ahead*, i.e., which pertains to faith in Christ or greater merits or heavenly things: "They go from strength to strength" (Ps. 84:5). He says *straining forward,* because a person who wishes to take anything must exert himself as much as he can. But the heart should stretch itself by desire: "The desire for wisdom leads to a kingdom" (Wis. 6:20). *For the prize,* which is the reward only of those who run: "In a race all the runners compete, but only one receives the prize" (1 Cor. 9:24); to this prize destined for me by God, namely, *of the upward call of God:* "Those whom he predestined he also called" (Rom. 8:30), and this *in Christ Jesus,* i.e., by faith in Christ.

3-3

15 Let those of us who are mature be thus minded; and if in anything you are otherwise minded, God will reveal that also to you. 16 Only let us hold true to what we have attained. 17 Brethren, join in imitating me, and mark those who so live as you have an example in us. 18 For many, of whom I have often told you and now tell you even with tears, live as enemies of the cross of Christ. 19 Their end is destruction, their god is the belly, and they glory in their shame, with minds set on earthly things. 20 But our commonwealth is in heaven, and from it we await a Savior, the Lord Jesus Christ, 21 who will change our lowly body to be like his glorious body, by the power which enables him even to subject all things to himself.

Above he showed how he was wanting in final perfection; now he urges others to have the same attitude: first, he gives an exhortation; secondly, what is necessarily expected of them (3:16).

He says: *Let those of us who are mature be thus minded,* namely, think what I think, i.e., that I am not perfect. But if we are perfect, how can we think that we are not perfect? I answer that some are perfect with the perfection of this life, but not with the perfection of the life of heaven, namely, when their entire intention will be actually borne toward God; but in this life they are perfect habitually when they do nothing contrary to God.

He says, *those of us,* because the more perfect a person is the more imperfect he considers himself to be: "I had heard of thee by the hearing of the ear, but now my eye sees thee; therefore I despise myself, and repent in dust and ashes" (Job 42:5); "Solid food is for the mature, for those who have their faculties trained by practice to distinguish good from evil" (Heb. 5:14).

And if in anything you are otherwise minded, God will reveal that also to you. Four renditions of this are found in a Gloss: the first two are more literal. One is this: I say that you should think as I do, namely, that you are imperfect; yet if you think otherwise, i.e., better of yourselves than I do of myself, this very thing has been granted to you by divine revelation: and when something loftier is revealed to you than to me, I will not contradict but will yield to your revelation. Nevertheless, I do not want you to separate from the unity of the Church because of this revelation; but in unity, let us hold *true to what we have attained.* This unity consists in the unity of the truth of faith and the rectitude of good action; and both must be preserved: "Mend your ways, heed my appeal, agree with one another, live in peace" (2 Cor. 13:11). And the same holds for a good life and good actions: "Peace and mercy be upon all who walk by this rule, upon the Israel of God "Gal. 6:16). Or another way: I say that if on account of ignorance or weakness you think otherwise than the truth holds, let us admit it humbly and do not defend it stubbornly: "Thou hast hidden these things from the wise and understanding and revealed them to babes" (Mt. 11:25). Or another way: I say that we should be of the same mind, namely, that we have not yet made it our own; but if in anything you are now otherwise minded than you will be in the future, because "now we see in a mirror dimly, but then face to face" (1 Cor. 13:12), *God will reveal* it in the future: "The voice of the Lord shakes the wilderness, . . . and strips the forests bare; and in his temple all cry Glory!" (Ps. 29:9). Or another way: Whether you understand dimly here, or clearly in the future, *God will reveal that,* because faith is from God. *Only let us hold true to what we have attained.*

Then when he says, *join in imitating me,* he urges them to

imitate him and others, but to avoid the wicked: first, he makes his point; secondly, he gives the reason (3:18).

He says, therefore: Because I regard these things as dung, that I may gain Christ, *brethren, join in imitating me* in this: "The sheep hear his voice" (Jn. 10:3). I am the shepherd; you are my sheep by imitating me: "Be imitators of me, as I am of Christ" (1 Cor. 11:1), *and mark,* i.e., carefully consider, *those who so live as you have an example in us.* And you can tell from my example and doctrine: "Set the believers an example in speech and conduct, in love, in faith, in purity (1 Tim. 4:12); "Being examples to the flock" (1 Pet. 5:3).

Then when he says, that *many live as enemies of the cross of Christ,* he gives the reason for his admonition: first, on the part of those to be avoided; secondly, of those to be followed (3:20). But lest this admonition seem to proceed from hatred: first, he mentions his affection; secondly, he describes the ones to be avoided (3:18b).

He says, therefore: I say that the ones to follow should be watched, because some walk otherwise, namely, from bad to worse: "They walk about in darkness" (Ps. 82:5). *Of whom I have often told you,* when I was with you, *and now tell you even with tears* of compassion: "O that my head were waters and my eyes a fountain of tears, that I might weep day and night for the slain of the daughter of my people!" (Jer. 9:1). He gives the reason for this when he says, *enemies of the cross of Christ.* First, he describes them from their work; secondly, from their intention (3:19). In regard to the first: first, he mentions their work; secondly, he shows the results of their work (3:19).

Their work is to practice enmity against the cross of Christ, namely, those who say that no one can be saved without observing the ceremonies of the Law, in which they nullify the power of the cross of Christ: "For the word of the cross is folly to those who are perishing, but to us who are being saved it is the power of God" (1 Cor. 1:18). And what will be the result? Certainly to us life through the cross of Christ; but to the others the opposite, because they incur death. Hence he says, *their end is destruction,* i.e., eternal death.

Then he describes their intention: first, he reveals their intention; secondly, the result of that intention (3:19). He says: *their god is the belly.* As if to say: they spread this doctrine, namely, that the ceremonies of the Law must be observed, for their own gain and glory to satisfy their belly: "For such persons do not serve our Lord Christ, but their own belly, and by fair and flattering words they deceive the hearts of the simpleminded" (Rom. 16:18); "All the toil of man is for his mouth, yet his appetite is not satisfied" (Eccl. 6:7). Hence he says *god,* because it is peculiar to God to be the first principle and the ultimate end; hence those who have something as an end have it as their God. Furthermore, they seek their own glory against what is stated in John (8:50): "Yet I do not seek my own glory; there is One who seeks it and he will be the judge." The result will be *their shame:* "I will change their glory into shame" (Ho. 4:7). This is the way things will turn out for those whose minds are fixed on earthly things, i.e., those whom earthly things please and who seek them. They will be ashamed because their state passes; "If you live according to the flesh you will die" (Rom. 8:13).

Then he describes the ones to be imitated when he says, *our commonwealth is in heaven.* First, he describes the heavenly commonwealth in them; secondly, their expectation (3:20b); thirdly, its usefulness (3:21).

He says: they seek earthly things, but not we, because *our commonwealth is in heaven,* i.e., is made perfect by contemplation: "We look not to the things that are seen but to the things that are unseen; for the things that are seen are transient, but the things that are unseen are eternal" (2 Cor. 4:18); and by affection, because we love only heavenly things; and by our actions, in which there is a representation of heaven: "Just as we have borne the image of the man of dust, we shall also bear the image of the man of heaven" (1 Cor. 15:49).

But why is our commonwealth there? Because that is the source from which we expect the most help: "I lift up my eyes to the hills from whence my help comes" (Ps. 121:1); "For where your treasure is there will your heart be also" (Mt. 6:21). Hence he says, *and from it we await a Savior:* "Blessed are the eyes that look for him" (Is. 30:18); "Be like men who are waiting for their master to come home from the marriage feast, so that they may open to him at once when he comes and knocks" (Lk. 12:36).

This coming involves three things: first, the general resurrection; hence he says, *who will change our lowly,* because it is subject to death, *body:* "Man, who is a maggot, and the son of man, who is a worm" (Job 25:6); "What is sown is perishable, what is raised is imperishable. It is sown in dishonor, it is raised in glory. It is sown in weakness, it is raised in power" (1 Cor. 15:42). This abject body *He will change [reform],* i.e., reduce it to His form: "He who raised Christ Jesus from the dead will give life to your mortal bodies also through his Spirit which dwells in you" (Rom. 8:11).

Secondly, the imitation of the saints; hence he says, *to be like his glorious body.* The body of Christ, of course, is glorified by the glory of His divinity; and He merited this by His passion. Therefore, whoever shares in the power of the divinity by grace and imitates the passion of Christ shall be glorified: "He who conquers, I will grant him to sit with me on my throne, as I myself conquered and sat down with my Father on his throne" (Rev. 3:21); "We shall be like him" (1 Jn. 3:2); "Then the righteous will shine like the sun in the kingdom of their Father" (Mt. 13:43). Thirdly, the power by which He does this: *by the power* of his Godhead, i.e., by the power in Him *which enables him even to subject all things to himself:* for all will be subject to Christ; some unto salvation, and some unto punishment. Toward the first He will exercise mercy, and toward the second justice: "Thou hast given dominion over the works of thy hands" (Ps. 8:6); "For God has put all things in subjection under his feet" (1 Cor. 15:27); "Whatever the Father does, that the Son does likewise" (Jn. 5:19).

4–1

1 Therefore, my brethren, who I love and long for, my joy and crown, stand firm thus in the Lord, my beloved. 2 I entreat

Euodia and I entreat Syntyche to agree in the Lord. 3 And I ask you also, true yokefellow, help these women, for they have labored side by side with me in the gospel together with Clement and the rest of my fellow workers, whose names are in the book of life. 4 Rejoice in the Lord always; again I will say, Rejoice. 5 Let all men know your forbearance. The Lord is at hand. 6 Have no anxiety about anything, but in everything by prayer and supplication with thanksgiving let your requests be made known to God. 7 And the peace of God, which passes all understanding, will keep your hearts and your minds in Christ Jesus. 8 Finally, brethren, whatever is true, whatever is honorable, whatever is just, whatever is pure, whatever is lovely, whatever is gracious, if there is any excellence, if there is anything worthy of praise, think about these things. 9 What you have learned and received and heard and seen in me, do; and the God of peace will be with you.

Above, he proposed examples for them to follow; here in a moral exhortation he shows how they should conduct themselves: first, how they should act in the future; secondly, he commends them on the past (4:10). In regard to the first he does two things: first, he urges them to persevere in what they already have; secondly, to advance to something better (4:4). The first is divided into two parts: first, he gives them a general exhortation to persevere; secondly, he lays down special ways for definite persons (4:2). In regard to the first: first, he reminds them of his own affection; secondly, he gives the exhortation (4:1b).

He certifies his affection in five ways: first, by reason of the faith, by showing that he loves them; hence he says, *my brethren,* i.e., through faith: "You are all brethren" (Mt. 23:8); secondly, by reason of charity; hence he says, *whom I love:* "My beloved" (1 Cor. 10:14); thirdly, according to desire; hence he says, *and long for:* "God is my witness, how I yearn for you all" (supra 1:8). And I say *long for,* because I long for you or because you long for me. Fourthly, by joy; hence he says, *my joy,* and this because you are good: "A wise son makes a glad father" (Prov. 10:1); fifthly, by reason of future joy; hence he says, *and crown;* "For what is our hope or joy or crown of boasting before our Lord Jesus at his coming? Is it not you?" (1 Thess. 2:19).

Then when he says, *stand firm thus in the Lord,* he urges them to persevere, saying, *stand firm,* i.e., persevere, as I do; or continue as you are: "He who endures to the end will be saved" (Mt. 10:22).

Then when he says, *I entreat Euodia,* he gives the individual exhortations: first, in regard to concord; secondly, in regard to solicitude in helping (4:3). These two women, Euodia and Syntyche, ministered to the saints in Philippi, and perhaps there was some strife between them. Therefore, he urges them to be at peace: "Agree with one another" (2 Cor. 13:11).

Then when he says, *I ask you also, true yokefellow,* he asks a certain person to help certain other persons. He says, *yokefellow,* because he was a fellow preacher: "A brother helped is like a strong city" (Prov. 18:19). *Help these women, for they have labored side by side with me in the gospel together with Clement and the rest of my fellow workers.* And I ask this of all *whose names are in the book of life.* He says this in order not to offend the others whom he did not name. As if to say: It makes no difference if I do not write everyone's name, because they are written in a better place: "Rejoice and be glad" (Mt. 5:12).

According to a Gloss the book of life is the same as the predestination of the saints. They are the same reality but the ideas are different. It should be noted that in olden times it was a custom to write in a register the names of those appointed to some duty or dignity, as soldiers and senators, who were enrolled in the palace. Now all the predestined saints are chosen by God for something great, namely, eternal life; and this appointment is called predestination. The record of this appointment is called the book of life: and this record is in the divine memory, because inasmuch as He appoints, He predestines; inasmuch as He knows it unchangeably, it is called foreknowledge. Therefore, this foreknowledge about the predestined is called the book of life.

But is anyone ever erased from this book? I answer that some are enrolled absolutely, and others in a qualified sense. For some are absolutely predestined by God to obtain eternal life, and they are enrolled indelibly. Others are predestined to have eternal life not in itself, but in its cause, inasmuch as they are ordained to justice for the present; and such persons are said to be erased from the book of life when they fall away from justice in this life.

Then when he says, *Rejoice in the Lord,* he urges them to make more progress: first, he prepares their mind to make more progress; secondly, he arranges their activity (4:8). In regard to the first he prepares their mind in regard to three things: first, in regard to spiritual joy; secondly, in regard to spiritual rest (4:6); thirdly, in regard to peace (4:7). In regard to the first: first, he describes what our joy should be; secondly, he discloses the cause of joy (4:5b).

Anyone who desires to make progress must have spiritual joy: "A cheerful heart is a good medicine" (Prov. 17:22). The Apostle touches on four characteristics of true joy; first, it must be right, this happens when it concerns the proper good of man, which is not something created, but God: "But for me it is good to be near God; I have made the Lord God my refuge" (Ps. 73:28). Therefore, it is right, when there is joy in the Lord; hence he says, *in the Lord:* "The joy of the Lord is your strength" (Neh. 8:10). Secondly, it is continuous; hence he says, *always,* "Rejoice always" (1 Thess. 5:16). This happens when it is not interrupted by sin, for then it is continuous. But sometimes it is interrupted by temporal sadness, which signifies the imperfection of joy. For when a person rejoices perfectly, his joy is not interrupted, because he cares little about things that do not last; that is why he says *always.* Thirdly, it should be multiple, for if you rejoice in God, you will rejoice in His incarnation: "I bring you good news of a great joy, which will come to all the people; for to you is born this day in the city of David a Savior" (Lk. 2:10); and in your own activity: "When justice is done, it is a joy to the righteous" (Prov. 21:15); and in your contemplation: "Companionship with her has no bitterness" (Wis. 8:16). Again, if you rejoice in your good, you will be prepared to rejoice in the good of others; if you rejoice in the present, you are prepared to rejoice in the future; hence he says, *again I will say, rejoice*. Fourthly, it should be moderate and not flooded with pleasures, as happens in worldly joy; hence he says, *let all men know your forbearance*. As if to say: Your joy should be so moderated that it will not degenerate into dissoluteness: "The people continued feasting in Jerusalem before the sanctuary" (Judith 16:20). He says, *let all men know*, as if to say: Your life should be so moderate in externals, that it offends the gaze of no one; for that would hinder your manner of life.

Then when he says, *the Lord is at hand,* he touches on the cause of joy. For a man rejoices when his friend is near. But the Lord is near with the presence of His majesty: "He is not far from each one of us" (Acts 17:27); He is also near in His flesh: "But now in Christ Jesus you who once were far off have been brought near in the blood of Christ" (Eph. 2:13). Again He is near through indwelling grace: "Draw near to God and he will draw near to you" (Jas. 4:8); and by His clemency in hearing: "The Lord is near to all who call upon him" (Ps. 145:18); and by His reward: "Its time is close at hand and its days will not be prolonged" (Is. 13:22).

Then when he says, *have no anxiety,* he shows that our minds should be at rest: first, that anxiety is uncalled for; secondly, what should take its place in our mind (4:6b).

It was fitting to add *have no anxiety* [*solicitude*] after saying that the Lord is at hand. As if to say: He will grant everything; hence there is no need to be anxious: "Do not be anxious about your life, what you shall eat or what you shall drink, nor about your body, what you shall put on" (Mt. 6:25).

But this seems to be contrary to what is stated in Romans (12:8): "He that rules, [do so] with solicitude." I answer that anxiety or solicitude sometimes suggests diligence in seeking what is lacking; and this is commendable and opposed to negligence. Sometimes it suggests anxiety of spirit with a lack of hope and with the fear of not obtaining that about which one is anxious. Such anxiety the Lord forbids in Matthew (6:25), because no one should despair, as though the Lord will not grant what is necessary. But in place of anxiety we should have recourse to God: "Cast all your anxieties on him, for he cares about you" (1 Pet. 5:7). And this is done by praying; hence he says, *but in everything let your requests be made known to God.*

It is fitting, after he says *the Lord is at hand,* to speak of petition, for it is customary to make petitions of a new lord on his arrival. He mentions four things required in every prayer. First, that prayer implies the ascent of the mind to God; therefore he says, *by prayer:* "The prayer of the humble pierces the clouds, and he will not be consoled until it reaches the Lord; he will not desist until the Most High visits him" (Si. 35:17). Secondly, it should be accompanied by confidence of obtaining, and this from God's mercy: "We do not present our supplications before thee on the ground of our righteousness, but on the grounds of thy great mercy" (Dan. 9:18); therefore, he says, *and supplication,* which is an appeal to God's grace and holiness; hence it is the prayer of a person humbling himself: "The poor use entreaties" (Prov. 18:23). We do this when we say: "Through your passion and cross. . . ." Thirdly, because a person who is ungrateful for past benefits does not deserve to receive new ones, he adds, *with thanksgiving:* "Give thanks in all circumstances" (1 Thess. 5:18). Fourthly, prayer is a petition; so he says, *let your requests be made known to God:* "Ask, and it will be given you" (Matt. 7:7). If we reflect, we will notice that all the prayers of the Church contain these four marks: first of all, God is invoked; secondly, the divine benefits are thankfully acknowledged; thirdly, a benefit is requested; and finally, the supplication is made: "Through our Lord. . . ."

But it should be noted that he says, *let your requests be made known to God.* Does not the Lord know them? This is explained in three ways in a Gloss: first, *let them be made known,* i.e., approved in God's presence and counted worthy and holy: "Let my prayer be counted as incense before thee" (Ps. 141:2). Or *let them be made known* to ourselves, that is, let us recognize that they always reach God. As if to say: "But when you pray, go into your room and shut the door and pray to your Father who is in secret; and your Father who sees in secret will reward you" (Matt. 6:6). Or, *let them be made known* to those who are with God, i.e., the angels, through whose ministry they are brought to God, not because He does not know them, but because they intercede for us: "The smoke of the incense rose with the prayers of the saints from the hand of the angel before God" (Rev. 8:4).

Then when he says, *and the peace of God . . . will keep your hearts,* he asks that peace descend on the soul now instructed by the things said above. He asks this as though he were entreating. Peace, according to Augustine, is the tranquility of order: for the disturbance of order is the destruction of peace. This tranquility of order is considered from three aspects: first, insofar as it exists in the principle of order, namely, in God: "For there is no authority except from God, and those that exist have been instituted by God. Therefore he who resists the authorities resists what God has appointed" (Rom. 13:1). From that profound source in which peace exists it flows first into the beatified, in whom there is no disturbance either of guilt or of punishment; then it flows into saintly men: the holier he is, the less his mind is disturbed: "Great peace have those who love thy law (Ps. 119:165). But it is more perfect in the beatified: "Behold, I will extend prosperity to her like a river, and the wealth of the nations like an overflowing stream" (Is. 66:12). Now because God alone can deliver the heart from all disturbance, it is necessary that it come from Him; hence he says, *of God:* and this, inasmuch as peace considered in that source *passes all* created *understanding,* as it is stated in 1 Timothy (6:16): "Who alone dwells in unapproachable light"; "Behold, God is great, and we know him not; the number of his years is unsearchable" (Job 36:26). As it exists in heaven, it surpasses all the knowledge of the angels; but as it exists in the saints on earth, it surpasses all the knowledge of those who lack grace: "To him who conquers I will give some of the hidden manna, and I will give him a white stone" (Rev. 2:17).

And the peace, therefore, *will keep your hearts,* i.e., your affections, so that you will never depart from the good in anything: "Keep your heart with all vigilance; for from it flow the springs of life" (Prov. 4:23); *and your minds,* so that they not deviate from the truth in anything. And this, *in Christ Jesus,* by whose love your affections are kept from evil and by whose faith your mind continues in the truth.

Then when he says, *finally brethren,* he puts order into their activity by urging them to do good; first, he mentions the object of action, namely, the good which is done; secondly, the mover to action; thirdly, the act itself; fourthly, the fruit of the act.

These four things are mentioned here. For the object of a good act is either the object of the intellect or of the affections: the object of the intellect is the true; the object of the affections is the good. Hence he says, *finally brethren,* i.e., since you are so minded, think of *whatever is true* through faith: "Love truth and peace" (Zech. 8:19). In regard to an object of the affections, certain characteristics must be present of necessity in a good act, and others are over and above. Of necessity are three things: first, that it be good in itself; hence he says, *whatever is honorable [chaste]:* "But the wisdom from above is first pure" (Jas. 3:17); secondly, that it be directed to one's neighbor; hence he says, *whatever is just:* "Blessed are those who hunger and thirst for righteousness [justice], for they shall be satisfied" (Matt. 5:6); thirdly, ordained to God; hence he says, *whatever is pure [holy]:* "That we might serve him without fear, in holiness and righteousness before him all the days of our life" (Lk. 1:74). The characteristics over and above what is necessary are twofold: first, that it lead to friendship; secondly, that it preserve one's good reputation. As to the first he says, *whatever is lovely,* i.e., leading to mutual friendship: "Do not shrink from visiting a sick man, because for such deeds you will be loved" (Si. 7:35); "There is a friend who sticks closer than a brother" (Prov. 18:24). As to the second he says, *whatever is gracious [of good fame].* For many things can be done with a good conscience, but must be omitted for the sake of one's reputation: "Have regard for your name, since it will remain for you longer than a thousand great stores of gold" (Si. 41:12).

The mover to action is twofold: first, the impulse given by a habit existing within oneself; secondly, discipline or instruction learned from someone else. As to the first he says, *if there is any excellence,* i.e., any habit of virtue in you, let it incline you to this: "Rich men furnished with resources, living peaceably in their habitations" (Si. 44:6). As to the second he says, *if there is [any discipline] anything worthy of praise,* i.e., praiseworthy knowledge, in you, do good: "Teach me good judgment and knowledge" (Ps. 119:66). He explains what that knowledge is when he says, *think about these things,* namely, *what you have learned* from my teaching: "Learn from me; for I am gentle and lowly in heart" (Matt. 11:29); "When you received the word of God which you heard from us, you accepted it not as the word of men but as what it really is, the word of God, which is at work in you believers" (1 Thess. 2:13); and *what you have seen* from my example. Thus the mover to action and its object are clear.

But because a discipline is obtained through doctrine, one must first acquire it; hence he says, *think about these things.* Then he must assent to it; hence he says, *what you have learned and received.* Furthermore, it is acquired by hearing and sight; hence he says, *what you have heard and seen.* But there are two kinds of good act: one is internal, and he mentions it when he says, *think about these things:* ["Meditate on these things"] (1 Tim. 4:15); the other is external: *do:* "Learn to do good; cease to do evil" (Is. 1:16).

The fruit is God, hence he says, *the peace of God will be with you.* As if to say: If you do all these things, God will be with you: "Live in peace, and the God of love and peace will be with you" (2 Cor. 13:11).

4–2

10 I rejoice in the Lord greatly that now at length you have revived your concern for me; you were indeed concerned for me, but you had no opportunity. 11 Not that I complain of want; for I have learned, in whatever state I am, to be content. 12 I know how to be abased, and I know how to abound; in any and all circumstances I have learned the secret of facing plenty and hunger, abundance and want. 13 I can do all things in him who strengthens me. 14 Yet it was kind of you to share

my trouble. 15 And you Philippians yourselves know that in the beginning of the gospel, when I left Macedonia, no church entered into partnership with me in giving and receiving except you only; 16 for even in Thessalonica you sent me help once and again. 17 Not that I seek the gift; but I seek the fruit which increases to your credit. 18 I have received full payment, and more; I am filled, having received from Epaphroditus the gifts you sent, a fragrant offering, a sacrifice acceptable and pleasing to God. 19 And my God will supply every need of yours according to his riches in glory in Christ Jesus. 20 To our God and Father be glory for ever and ever. Amen. 21 Greet every saint in Christ Jesus. The brethren who are with me greet you. 22 All the saints greet you, especially those of Caesar's household. 23 The grace of the Lord Jesus Christ be with your spirit.

Above, the Apostle showed how the faithful should conduct themselves in regard to the future; here he commends them for past benefits conferred by them. First, he gives the commendation; secondly, he ends the epistle with a prayer and a greeting (4:19). In regard to the first he does two things: first, he commends them for past favors; secondly, he explains the favor more fully (4:11). The first is divided into three parts: first, he expresses the joy he experienced from their favor; secondly, he commends their favor (4:10); thirdly, he excuses their slowness (4:10).

He says, therefore: I urged you to rejoice; but now *I rejoice*, because of what you have done and for the things themselves, but I do so *in the Lord:* "I will rejoice in the Lord, I will joy in the God of my salvation" (Hab. 3:18). *I rejoice,* I say, *greatly,* because of my children.

Then he states the reason for his joy when he says, *that now at length you have revived your concern for me [your concern has flourished].* Good works are acts of mercy and they are called flowers, because just as the fruit is produced after the flower, so from acts of mercy the fruit of eternal life is received: "My blossoms became glorious and abundant fruit" (Si. 24:17). Therefore, when a good work is interrupted and then resumed, it is said to flower again. But they once provided for the Apostle, and now they provided again; therefore he says, *you have revived your concern for me. [it has flourished again]*. He explains this when he says, *you were indeed concerned for me*, i.e., sympathized with me: "It is right for me to feel thus about you all" (*supra* 1:7); "You are to be called the king's friend and you are to take our side and keep friendship with us" (1 Mac. 10:20); or *you were indeed concerned for me*, namely, when you provided for me. And you have done this *now at length*, i.e., although it is late, you have done something.

Then when he says, *but you had no opportunity*, he excuses their slowness. As if to say: I do not lay it to negligence but to necessity, because you were busy with the tribulations you suffered: "Much labor was created for every man" (Si. 40:1).

Then when he says, *not that I complain of want*, he begins to comment on the favor they did. First, why it is a reason for joy; secondly, he mentions a past favor; thirdly, he commends it (4:18). In regard to the first he does three things: first, he excludes a supposed reason for joy; secondly, he mentions his own constancy of mind (4:11b); thirdly, he approves their kindness (4:14).

He says, therefore: I do not rejoice in the fact that you relieved my want, although it was serious: "I have tried you in the furnace of affliction [poverty]" (Is. 48:10); yet it depresses only the spirit of those who are delighted with riches, or glory in their substance. Therefore, the Apostle is not saddened by poverty. The reason for this is his constancy of mind, which he mentions first; and secondly its cause. First, he mentions his constancy in a particular case; secondly, universally in all things (4:12).

He says, therefore: I do not fear poverty, because *I have learned in whatever state I am, to be content*. For nothing so well demonstrates the mind of a perfect wise man as knowing how to make use of every state in which he finds himself. For just as a good leader in any army is the one who acts as circumstances require, and a good tanner is one who makes the best leather from each hide; so he is perfect who knows how to make the best of his state: if he is in lofty state, he is not lifted up; if in the lowest state, he is not dejected. Therefore he says, *I have learned in whatever state I am, to be content:* "The Lord God has opened my ear and I was not rebellious, I turned not backward" (Is. 50:5). If I have a little, it is enough; if I have much, I know how to be moderate.

He explains himself, saying: *I know how to be abased.* Now, abasement sometimes denotes a virtue: "He who humbles himself will be exalted" (Lk. 18:14); and sometimes a low condition: "His feet were hurt with fetters, his neck was put in a collar of iron" (Ps. 105:18). This is what he means when he says, *I know how to be abased,* i.e., how to endure a lowly condition with equanimity, as is becoming. And because men are exalted by riches and humbled by poverty, there is danger in each of these conditions: because abundance may raise the mind against God, and poverty withdraw it; hence it is stated in Proverbs (30:8): "Give me neither poverty nor riches." But the Apostle knows how to employ virtue in both; therefore, *in any and all circumstances,* i.e., in all places, affairs, states and conditions I have learned the secret: "In all things let us conduct ourselves as God's ministers" (2 Cor. 6:4).

Then when he says, *I can do all things,* he reveals the cause of his constancy saying, *I can do all things in him who strengthens me.* As if to say: I would not be able to endure want, unless the hand of God supported me: "The hand of the Lord was strong upon me" (Ez. 3:14); "They who wait for the Lord shall renew their strength, they shall mount up with wings like eagles, they shall run and not be weary, they shall walk and not faint" (Is. 40:31).

But are the things we sent superfluous, since you know how to endure want? No, because although I know how to suffer need, you ought not withdraw your help: "Contribute to the needs of the saints" (Rom. 12:13); "You had compassion on the prisoners" (Heb. 10:34).

Secondly, he recalls a past favor; *and you Philippians yourselves know.* For he had received nothing from certain ones, such as the Corinthians and Thessalonians, because the Corinthians were covetous and became annoyed when they ministered to him; and because the Thessalonians were given to idleness, he labored, giving them an example of work. Yet the Philippians were good, whether he was present or absent; hence he says in 2 Corinthians (11:8): "I robbed other churches by accepting support from them in order to serve you." *No church entered into partnership with me in giving* temporal things *and receiving* spiritual things *except you only.* "If we have sown spiritual good among you, is it too much if we reap your material benefits?" (1 Cor. 9:11). *For even in Thessalonica you sent me help once and again.* This is the reason why the Pope can take from one church to help another; but not without cause.

Not that I seek the gift. Here it should be noted that when a person gives something to someone else, two things should be considered: the substance of the gift and the merit of the donor. One who takes joy in temporal things rejoices in the substance of the gift and looks only for donors; this is a hireling. But one who looks at the merit of the donor looks for the fruit of virtue and justice; such a one is a shepherd. *But I seek the fruit which increases to your credit.* He says, *increases,* because they gave more than they were required: for some gave while he was among them, but others even gave while he was in Rome. *I am filled, having received the gifts you sent, a fragrant offering, a sacrifice acceptable and pleasing to God.* "A pleasing odor to the Lord" (Lev. 4:31). For the devotion of the offerer is a sweet odor to God; and of all offerings an alms is very beneficial: "Do not neglect to do good and to share what you have, for such sacrifices are pleasing to God" (Heb. 13:16).

Then when he says, *[may] my God will supply every need of yours,* he brings the epistle to a close with a prayer: *[may] my God.* There is one God of all men by creation and power; but He is *mine,* because I serve Him in a special way: "For God is my witness whom I serve" (Rom. 1:9). May He supply all your needs, because you have supplied mine. The Lord can do this because He abounds in riches: "The same Lord is Lord of all and bestows his riches upon all who call upon him" (Rom. 10:12); hence he says, *according to his riches.* And this, *in glory,* because in glory all his desires will be satisfied: "As for me, I shall behold thy face in righteousness" (Ps. 17:15). ["I shall be satisfied when your glory shall appear"] (Ps. 102:5).

And this, *in Christ Jesus,* i.e., through Christ: "By which he has granted to us his precious and very great promises" (2 Pet. 1:4). For all these things, *to our God,* to the Trinity, *and to our Father be glory:* "To the only God, be honor and glory for ever and ever" (1 Tim. 1:17).

Then he gives the greeting when he says, *greet every saint in Christ Jesus,* i.e., those who believe in Christ, because they were sanctified by Christ: "So Jesus also suffered outside the gate in order to sanctify the people through his own blood" (Heb. 13:12); *especially those of Caesar's household.* This shows that he converted many from Caesar's household: "It has become known throughout the whole court and to all the rest" (*supra* 1:13).

But although it is stated in Matthew (11:8) that those in soft garments are in the houses of kings, nevertheless to help the good and to hinder the wicked, it seems to be lawful for holy men to dwell in the courts of kings, but not for the sake of voluptuous pleasures and desires. Therefore, he says, *those of Caesar's household,* in order to arouse their joy and faith.

Then he writes a greeting in his own hand: *The grace of the Lord Jesus Christ be with your spirit.*